THE ALIPORE BOMB CASE

Published by
NIYOGI BOOKS
(A unit of Niyogi Offset Pvt. Ltd.)
D-78, Okhla Industrial Area, Phase-I
New Delhi-110 020, India

Tel: 91-11-26816301, 26813350, 51, 52
Fax: 91-11-26810483, 26813830

email: niyogioffset@bol.net.in
www.niyogibooks.com

Designed by: Write Media

ISBN: 978-81-89738-31-0

Year of Publication: 2008
Reprint: 2024

Printed at: Niyogi Offset Pvt. Ltd, New Delhi, India

THE ALIPORE BOMB CASE

A Historic Pre-Independence Trial

Noorul Hoda

Edited by
Shyam Banerji

NIYOGI BOOKS

Contents

Liberty of Thought and Action

Liberty of thought and action is the only condition of life, of growth and well-being. Where it does not exist the man, the race, the nation must go down. Any man or class or caste or nation or institution which bars the power of free thought and action of individual—even so long as that power does not injure others—is devilish and must go down. Whatever retards the onward progress or helps the downward fall is vice; whatever helps in coming up and becoming harmonised is virtue.

My idea is to bring to the door of the meanest, the poorest, the noble ideas that the human race has developed both in and out of India, and let them think for themselves. We preach neither social equality nor inequality but that every being has the same right and insist upon freedom of thought and action in every way. Liberty is the first condition.

The Lord's blessings on you all! His powers be in you all—as I believe it is already. "Wake up, stop not until the goal is reached," say the Vedas—up, up the long night is passing, the day is approaching, the wave has risen, nothing will be able to resist its tidal fury. The spirit, young ones, the spirit; the love, brave ones, the love, the faith, the belief; and fear not. The greatest sin is fear …

Do not be afraid of a small beginning. Have you love? You are omnipotent. Are you perfectly unselfish? If so you are irresistible. It is the Lord who protects his children in the depths of the sea. Your country requires heroes. Be heroes.

The present enthusiasm is only a little patriotism, it means nothing. If it is true and genuine you will find, within a short time, hundreds of heroes coming forward and carrying on the work.

Swami Vivekananda

From Bande Mataram, *1907*

Organised national resistance to existing conditions, whether directed against the system of Government as such or against some particular feature of it, has three courses open to it. It may attempt to make administration under existing conditions impossible by an organised passive resistance ... It may attempt to make administration under existing conditions impossible by an organised aggressive resistance in the shape of an untiring and implacable campaign of assassination and a confused welter of riots, strikes and agrarian risings all over the country ... The third course open to an oppressed nation is that of armed revolt, which instead of bringing existing conditions to an end by making their continuance impossible, sweeps them bodily out of existence. This is the old time-honoured method which the oppressed or enslaved have always adopted by preference in the past, and will adopt in the future if they see any chance of success; for it is the readiest and swiftest, the most thorough in its results, and demands the least powers of endurance and suffering and the smallest and briefest sacrifices. The choice by a subject nation of the means it will use for vindicating its liberty, is best determined by the circumstances of its servitude.

Aurobindo Ghose

13 April 1907

Long after this controversy is hushed in silence, long after this turmoil, this agitation ceases, long after he is dead and gone, he will be looked upon as the poet of patriotism, as the prophet of nationalism and the lover of humanity. Long after he is dead and gone, his words will be echoed and re-echoed, not only in India, but across distant seas and lands. Therefore, I say that the man in his position is not only standing before the bar of this court but before the bar of the High Court of History.

Chittaranjan Das
Aurobindo Ghose's Defence Counsel
in the Alipore Bomb Trial, 1909

Acknowledgements

I take this opportunity to express my sincere gratitude to all those who have helped me in the successful completion of this book.

I am immensely grateful to Mr. Nihar Roy, Director, Calcutta Police Museum, who provided valuable information on Douglas Kingsford, the Book Bomb, and also supplied the photographs of the objects connected with the Alipore Bomb Case from his museum.

I extend my sincere thanks to the National Archives of India for providing all the relevant papers and photographs of the persons who were connected with this trial. My thanks especially to Mr. K.K. Sharma, Assistant Director, and Mr. Jagmohan Jareda of the National Archives.

I would also like to thank Mr. Shyam Banerji for his masterly handling of the manuscript.

And no words are enough to express my appreciation and admiration for Mr. Bikash D. Niyogi and Mrs. Tultul Niyogi of Niyogi Books for publishing this book. They have significantly contributed to society by bringing out a memorable book.

Last, but not least, I am indebted to my family and friends for their support and encouragement.

Noorul Hoda
New Delhi
January, 2008

Editor's Note

Revisiting Ourselves

At sometime or another every human being relives his or her history. But almost as easily the march of time ensures that certain memories grow hazy and are soon lost forever.

As we move from one day to the next caught up in the race to outdo the other, we often forget that perhaps we would not have been where we are had someone, somewhere—maybe sometime way back in the past—not made a huge sacrifice for us. That someone could be our parents, our ancestors, or even a dear friend ... someone who took that one defining step that helped to place us on the highway of success.

Imagine forgetting the contribution of such a person as we bask in the halo of our new-found achievements. Similarly, imagine a considerable part of the nation forgetting the contribution of an entire generation of brave-hearts who were instrumental in giving back to us our first and foremost right ... our freedom!

Kanai Dutt, Satyendranath Bose, Charu Charan Bose, Upendra Nath Banerjee, Indu Bhushan Roy, Ullaskar Dutt, Basant Biswas and Ratan Lahiri were bright, young men who sacrificed their lives for India. Yet today, except for the renaming of Muraripukur Lane (the street where the Ghose family house Bagan Bari or Garden House lies) to Barin Ghose Sarani, these martyrs are sadly forgotten.

If we relegate our national heroes and freedom fighters to oblivion, we stand to be sentenced harshly by the jury of time. History is a ruthless taskmaster. When it passes its sentence, there can be no further appeal.

This is just one of the many reasons to celebrate the publication of *The Alipore Bomb Case: A Historic Pre-Independence Trial,* a timely and necessary retelling of one of the most famous legal cases in Indian history.

Working on the editorial planning of *The Alipore Bomb Case* was akin to setting off on an illuminating and inspiring journey. This book takes its inspiration from some of the rarest documents in the Indian national archives.

In presenting these documents, we decided to maintain a uniformity of spelling and nomenclature as far as possible. *The Alipore Bomb Case* is a fascinating window into a lesser-known era of India's struggle for freedom.

If *The Alipore Bomb Case* succeeds in illuminating a forgotten era and transports the reader back in space and time, this book would have served its purpose.

Shyam Banerji
New Delhi
January, 2008

Introduction

A Journey Begins

In understanding Indian culture and studying the vast ocean of India's cultural evolution, I have concentrated on the political, social and religious aspects of India. The judicial aspect of culture (especially the defining role of jurisprudence and the inter-relation between social, political and judicial values) and the judicial milestones that have shaped Indian history and thought have remained largely ignored or unexplored.

The study of judicial history always puts an introspective mirror in front of us. It is a mirror that helps us understand ourselves. It is in this context that the trials of Indian freedom fighters emerge as a very important aspect of India's cultural history—an aspect that needs to be made known to all. At the same time, it is also important to get the inside picture of how the judiciary facilitated the British imperial design as India struggled for its freedom.

The Alipore Bomb Case, the subject of this book, is one of the most sensational cases of India, particularly in this context. India's fight for freedom is a saga of supreme sacrifices.

The achievement of freedom in 1947 was not an overnight victory. It was the culmination of a long-drawn battle in which many people laid down their lives for their motherland.

This book is closely connected with India's struggle for freedom and focuses on the immediate and not so immediate causes and incidents that led to the occurrence of the landmark case. It is also a revealing statement on the role played by many known and unknown people in India's independence struggle. People who loved the country selflessly; people who martyred themselves with songs on their lips; people ... many of whom have been sadly forgotten!

My inspiration to work on this book stemmed from an innate desire to rekindle the memory of these brave souls and pay regards to the great sons of the soil who sacrificed their lives for their country.

Sri Aurobindo Ghose, one of the accused in the Alipore Bomb Case

Sri Aurobindo Ghose, one of the accused in the Alipore Bomb Case, wrote in his famous article titled *The Morality of Boycott*:

> Love has a place in politics, but it is the love of one's country, for one's countrymen, for the glory, greatness and happiness of the race, the divine *ananda* of self-immolation for one's fellows, the ecstasy of relieving their sufferings, the joy of seeing one's blood for country and freedom, the bliss of union in death with the fathers of the race. The feeling of almost physical delight in the touch of the mother-soil, of the winds that blow from Indian seas, of the rivers that stream from Indian hills, in the hearing of Indian speech, music, poetry, in the familiar sights, sounds, habits, dress, manners of our Indian life, this is the physical root of that love.
>
> The pride in our past, the pain of our present, the passion for the future, are its trunk and branches. Self-sacrifice and self-forgetfulness, great service, high endurance for the country are its fruit. And the sap which keeps it alive is the realisation of the Motherhood of God in the country, the vision of the Mother, the knowledge of the Mother, the perpetual contemplation, adoration and service of the Mother.

The decline of the Mughals after the death of Aurangzeb in 1707 opened the doorway of political opportunities for European traders. Their frequent indulgence in Indian political affairs led to the creation of their sovereign authority in India; an authority that was highly exploitative and driven by commercial interests; an authority that, with time, became the virtual monopoly of the British East India Company and the British Crown.

Calcutta (now Kolkata) emerged as the first imperial capital of the British Government in India and British administration changed the social, political and economic balance of the country. The people of India always questioned the legitimacy and moral authority of British rule in India. This protest saw many battles and confrontations.

The media also played an important role in awakening the masses against the British atrocities. The government, in turn, unleashed tighter legislation to control them.

Raja Ram Mohan Roy wrote a spirited editorial in the last issue of his Persian weekly *Mirat-ul-Akhbar* on the occasion of the protest against the Press Act in 1823. In it, he argued in defence of the freedom of the press by quoting a Persian couplet that said:

Social reformer
Raja Ram Mohan Roy

The honour that has been purchased at the cost of a hundred drops of blood of the heart, O, Sire, do not sell that honour to the door-keeper for hoping to get a favour.

British imperialism in India was established with the help of Indian soldiers who were more faithful to British officers than their Indian kings. But, enraged by divisive and oppressive British policies, these Company sepoys decided to overthrow the government. This gave birth to the first milestone in our freedom struggle—the Revolt of 1857—which was led by the Company's soldiers and afterwards spearheaded by Rani Lakshmi Bai at Jhansi, Bakht Khan at Delhi, Nana Saheb and Tantiya Tope at Kanpur, Ahmadullah of Faizabad, among others. It was called the First War of Independence by Indians. The British named it the Sepoy Mutiny. Since the war was started, led and spearheaded by soldiers, I would like to name it as the Sepoy's Struggle for Independence. The Indian soldier-led revolutionary war was, however, preceded as well as followed by many other armed movements.

British rule in India from 1860 to 1908 was an era of famine and death. About 29 million Indians are estimated to have died due to poverty and starvation. The period was also marked by a renewed upsurge of imperialist control by the British, as seen in the reactionary policies of Viceroys such as Lytton, Dufferin and Curzon. This found response in the growth of a powerful nationalist struggle during the second half of the 19th century and the first half of the 20th century—a struggle rooted in the clash of interests between Indians and the British.

Against the backdrop of this increasing divide between the ruler and the ruled, which was fuelled by British policies, the Indian National Congress was born. As its moderate approach of constitutional reforms and welfare measures failed to satisfy the demands of those Indians who now wanted something more than just British lip service, there was frustration and anger. Out of this arose an extreme form of nationalism, first in Maharashtra and then in Bengal.

In 1905, Viceroy Lord Curzon partitioned Bengal into two provinces—Bengal and Eastern Bengal and Assam. It was a well-calculated strategy to create a rift among nationalists on the basis of religion, region and class; an attempt on the part of the government to subvert the nationalist movement. The move, at the very outset, was resented by all the nationalist leaders.

Subsequent events led to the launch of *swadeshi* and boycott, which became the battle cry for the nationalists. For the first time people from all sections of society participated in the movement and pledged to fight for *swaraj* or self-rule as a basic right. Nationalist newspapers played a major role in inciting public opinion against alien rule. The government tried to muffle the press through arrests and prosecutions.

During this period, a large number of young students joined the nationalist movement and adopted violence as a means to achieve freedom. Secret societies were formed with the aim of killing important British officials and their Indian sympathisers. It was around this time that an attempt was made at Muzaffarpur in Bihar, on the life of Douglas Kingsford, the ex-Magistrate of the Calcutta Presidency. The incident created a sensation in the British circles and it proved to be the benchmark for the beginning of a historic trial known as the Alipore Bomb Conspiracy Case—the central subject of this book.

The Alipore Bomb Case: A Historic Pre-Independence Trial is divided into four chapters. The first chapter deals with the decline of the Mughals and the gradual emergence of the British as the sovereign power in India. It gives a background of the divisive and oppressive policies of the British that led to the 1857 War, the subsequent developments, the division of Bengal in 1905, the events that followed in Bengal, the role of the print media in building public opinion and the emergence of secret societies in Bengal.

The second chapter focuses on the retaliation of the revolutionary groups. It touches upon some of the important attempts made on the lives of British officials, the attempt on the life of D.H. Kingsford by Khudiram Bose and Prafulla Chaki in Muzaffarpur and the accidental killing of two British ladies, the related chain of events, the suicide of Prafulla Chaki and the trial and sentencing of Khudiram Bose.

The third chapter talks about the after-effects of the Muzaffarpur incident; the raids and the arrest of several people associated with secret societies; their roles in various attempts on the lives of high profile British officials; their plans for overthrowing the British Government through revolutionary action; the trial of the accused persons and the judgement of the Alipore Sessions Court in the case that came to be known as the Alipore Bomb Conspiracy.

The fourth chapter picks up the thread of post-trial incidents; the growth of secret society networks and revolutionary activities in all parts of the country; the reaction of nationalist leaders; the decision of the British Government to revoke the partition of Bengal; the shift of the capital from Calcutta to Delhi in 1912 and the rise of the revolutionary movement in the next two decades.

Brief biographical sketches of the main players in the Alipore Bomb Conspiracy Case have been included in the end.

Noorul Hoda
New Delhi,
January, 2007

Chapter One

The Genesis

The turn of the 20th century was marked by a major development in many parts of the world. It saw several countries under the subjugation of European powers striving to free themselves from colonial bondage. India, which was reeling under the British imperial yoke, was one of the first to accelerate the wheel of freedom.

This book throws light on a less explored but extremely significant movement, popularly known as the revolutionary movement, in India's struggle for independence. It looks back at this turbulent period of Indian history through the window of a landmark trial officially known as the Alipore Bomb Conspiracy. A fiery testimony to the emotions that stirred the call for freedom, the trial brought into focus the lives, the resolute commitment and the valourous acts of many known and unknown revolutionaries. By bringing their personalities, beliefs and actions into the spotlight, the Alipore Bomb Conspiracy inspired the establishment of revolutionary organisations in other parts of India; those that shared an over-riding aim—the liberation of 'Mother India' from British rule!

Even a cursory look at the history of India shows that this ancient land has many faces to it. Unity, diversity, continuity and change have been its concurrent and constant companions. There were times when a large portion of the subcontinent was under the rule of one unifying empire. Conversely, there were times when the land was so disunited that foreign invaders found it an opportune source for rich pickings. Time and again, invaders came through the western passes. Some settled here, became Indians, ruled as kings and emperors and enriched the uniquely assimilative fabric of India. Others were drawn by India's fabled riches and came primarily to plunder, loot and then return to their homelands.

Standing at the crossroads of time, India was therefore impacted by many changes, achievements and influences. Dynastic fortunes

Mughal Emperor Aurangzeb, whose death in 1707 was followed by a period of anarchy

rose and fell, and with it the country also swayed between the upbeat of growth and prosperity and the downtrend of stagnation and misery.

For almost two centuries, the Mughals had contributed immensely to the artistic, cultural, economic and administrative development of India. The death of Aurangzeb, the last of the great Mughal emperors in 1707, however, proved to be a major blow to the edifice of united India. It was followed by anarchy and lawlessness.

In the absence of a strong central authority, the once powerful empire disintegrated into smaller, independent states. This disintegration eventually paved the way for the establishment of a new power from across the seas. A power that was not only alien in origin but also alien in its nature of governance—the British and their East India Company. Lured by the lucrative Indian trade, they were quick to grab the opportunity and when the time was ripe, they were also quick to change their garb and stay back as a relentlessly exploitative colonial power.

The origin of the British establishment in India can actually be traced back to the early 17th century when a liberal trading policy was introduced during the reign of Mughal Emperor Jahangir (1605-1627) to encourage trade and strengthen the exchange pattern.

A few years before the accession of Jahangir, Queen Elizabeth I of England had issued a Royal Charter on 31 December 1600 to establish what came to be famously known as the English East India Company. A joint stock company that enjoyed the royal privilege to trade in Indian waters, it initially found it difficult to make a dent in the Dutch-controlled East Indies' spice-trade but eventually it's ships began docking at Surat, which was established as a trade transit point in the year 1608.

Encouraged by the trade potential and the initial profits made by the Company, in 1609 King James I of England renewed the charter given to the Company for an indefinite period but added a clause that specified that the charter would cease to be in effect if the trade became unprofitable for three consecutive years. Wresting control over the East

Indies trade, however, necessitated regular battles with the Dutch and Portugese fleets. The English concluded that there had to be a more diplomatic way!

In 1615, Sir Thomas Roe, an emissary of King James I, visited the court of Jahangir with his eyes on a commercial treaty that could give the English East India Company exclusive rights to reside and build factories in Surat and other places on the Indian coastline. In return, the Company offered to provide the Emperor valuable goods and rarities from the European market. This mission was highly successful. Emperor Jahangir sent a letter to King James I in which he wrote:

> Upon which assurance of your royal love I have given my general command to all the kingdoms and ports of my dominions to receive all the merchants of the English nation as the subjects of my friend; that in what place soever they choose to live, they may have free liberty without any restraint; and at what port soever they shall arrive, that neither Portugal nor any other shall dare to molest their quiet; and in what city soever they shall have residence, I have commanded all my governors and captains to give them freedom answerable to their own desires; to sell, buy, and to transport into their country at their pleasure. For confirmation of our love and friendship, I desire your Majesty to command your merchants to bring in their ships of all sorts of rarities and rich goods fit for my palace; and that you be pleased to send me your royal letters by every opportunity, that I may rejoice in your health and prosperous affairs; that our friendship may be interchanged and eternal.

Mughal Emperor Jahangir introduced a liberal trading policy

The sympathetic attitude of the Emperor towards the new trading company boosted the morale of the English. After establishing strongholds in Surat and Madras in 1650, they also obtained a licence to trade in Bengal. A factory was established at Hughli the very next year. In 1690, Job Charnock established a factory that was fortified in 1698 and became famous as Fort William. The villages of Sutanati, Kalikata and Gobindpore were developed into a single area called Calcutta and soon became a trading hub for the British East India Company.

It did not take much time for the Company to widen its interests and start interfering in Indian polity and administration. King Charles II had

Robert Clive, who led the British in the decisive Battle of Plassey in 1757

already armed the Company with rights to acquire territory, mint money, command fortresses and troops, enter into war, alliance and peace treaties and also exercise civil and criminal jurisdiction over the acquired areas. The establishment of Fort William thus further strengthened the formidable and intimidating military strength already possessed by the Company. The field was now ripe for conflict and confrontation as the British coastal supremacy prepared to make its political inroads into the Indian heartland. The first battle that proved decisive for the establishment of British rule in India was the Battle of Plassey in 1757 in which British forces led by Robert Clive defeated Nawab Siraj-ud-daulah of Bengal. In a large measure, the victory was made possible by the treachery of the Nawab's general, Mir Jafar.

Another important battle that contributed to the strengthening of British power in India was the Battle of Buxar in 1764 between the British forces and the combined armies of Mir Kasim, the Nawab of Bengal; Shuja-ud-daulah, the Nawab of Awadh and Shah Alam II, the Mughal Emperor. On that fateful day on the banks of the Ganga at Buxar, a new era was engraved in the annals of Indian history. Victory in the battle gave the British the *diwani* or right to administer and collect the revenues of Bengal (which at that time included not just present-day West Bengal, but also almost the entire present-day Jharkhand, Bihar, Orissa and Bangladesh).

For the British, literally speaking, it was a huge stranglehold—a territorial stranglehold—that heralded the establishment of the rule of the British East India Company in the eastern part of the Indian subcontinent. Even many Britishers were surprised, because success in India had come more swiftly than they could have ever imagined.

British rule in India was fundamentally different from what the country and its people had experienced before. The British were here as imperial powers and their main objective was the political enslavement of India and the commercial exploitation of its resources. Consequently, the administration that developed tried to bring about fundamental changes in the social, political and economic condition of the country with the primary objective of reducing India to a subject colony at the economic disposal of its British imperial masters. Increasing consolidation of British power in India was accompanied by increasing British control over the lives of Indians and a systematic draining of the wealth of India for the benefit of Britain.

The exploitative measures adopted by the British were, however, not unaccompanied by opposition and protest from Indian quarters. Since the very beginning of British rule, the people of India questioned Britain's legitimacy and moral authority to impose alien rule over a sovereign people. This resentment cascaded into the Great Revolt of 1857, also known as the First War of Independence. The Revolt of 1857 was by no means the first revolt against British rule in India. In the hundred years between the defeat at Plassey in 1757 and the outburst of protest at Meerut in 1857, the soldiers of the Company had almost always been on a 'call to arms' in one part of the country or another. In Bengal, towards the end of the 18th century, they had to face starving peasants led by saffron-robed holy men in what is called the 'Sanyasi Rebellion'. Around the same time they had to deal with peasant rebellions in Tripura, Bengal and Mysore; troop mutinies in Vellore and Barrackpore; the Santhal revolt and the crusades of the Faraizis and Wahabis. However, upheavals like these were isolated, badly organised and thus easily suppressed. The same was to a large extent true of the various encounters that made up the Revolt of 1857.

First War of Independence, 1857

At the immediate level, the events of 1857 were sparked by some British actions that threatened the religious sanctities and caste conventions of Indian soldiers in the British Army. The introduction of the new Enfield rifle (with its greased cartridge) was one such example. The cartridges, which had to be bitten off before loading, were greased with a mix of animal fat—notably cow and pig fat—and this met with stiff resistance from Indian soldiers because the cow was sacrosanct to Hindus and the pig was taboo for Muslims. At a wider level, however, even people such as Benjamin Disraeli (who later became the Prime Minister of Great Britain) admitted that the root cause lay in the overall administration of the government that had alienated or alarmed almost every influential class in the country. The immediate military reasons apart, the fact remains that there was deep unrest among the population because it viewed

The arrest of Mughal Emperor Bahadur Shah Zafar

British actions as interference in, and contempt for, India's long established conventions and traditions.

A turning point in the history of the country, the Revolt of 1857 was crushed by the British with a heavy hand. The last rebels were defeated in Gwalior on 20 June 1858. In gory medieval tradition, many sentenced rebels were leashed to the mouths of cannons and blown to pieces by the British. It was a brutal fight on either side. Not surprisingly therefore, the British reprisal was equally brutal. Mughal Emperor Bahadur Shah Zafar, the titular head of the revolt, was captured and exiled to Rangoon (Myanmar) where he died in 1862.

On the face of it, the Revolt of 1857 remained confined to northern and central India, but it would be a fallacy to think that it did not stir the sentiments of a major part of the country. It was an event that left deep cracks on all aspects of future Indo-British relationships. The big visible change happened at the top. Opposition to the British East India Company and criticism of its handling of Indian affairs had already been building up in Britain. This culminated in the passing of the Act for Better Government of India in 1858. The Governor-General became a Viceroy representing the British Sovereign, and political authority passed from the hands of the Company to a Secretary of State for India who was to be responsible to the British Parliament. The East India Company's rule ended and India now came directly under the British Crown. Lord Canning had the unique distinction of being the British Governor-General of India and also the first Viceroy. In a few years the imperial wheel turned a full circle when Queen Victoria was proclaimed Empress of India in 1877.

However, down below—invisible to many—popular Indian discontent and nationalist feelings had started simmering stronger than ever before.

The British became more cautious and defensive about their Indian empire. The Queen's Proclamation Act of 1858 had confirmed the earlier treaties between the East India Company and the Indian princes and a general pardon had been granted to all offenders except those directly involved in the killing of British subjects. The Indian Army, which had been at the centre of the revolt, was thoroughly reorganised. The policy of ruthless conquests in India was set aside; perhaps it would be more apt to say that it was now not needed anymore.

Indian princes were given the assurance that their states would not be annexed. Their right to adopt heirs in the absence of natural successors—a right that had been usurped by Lord Dalhousie through his famous Doctrine of Lapse—was restored. Indians were also guaranteed full religious freedom and assured of appointments to high government positions without any discrimination. The Indian Councils Act, the High Courts Act and the Penal Code were passed in 1861. The expansion of the rail and telegraph network was taken up with strategic urgency.

The government initiated various welfare measures to win public confidence, but many in the Indian population had now wisened up enough to see through the veil of British promises. Bitterness and mistrust became the defining streaks of the post-1857 Indo-British relationship. As British chronicler Thomas Lowe put it in 1860:

> To live in India, now, was like standing on the verge of a volcanic crater, the sides of which were fast crumbling away from our feet, while the boiling lava was ready to erupt and consume us.

There was widespread discontent among farmers who were forced to produce cash crops that the British sold for profits that were never shared with the farmers. At the same time, Indians were also coerced to accept cheaper, machine-made British goods that destroyed indigenous cottage industries. India was being pushed by its colonial masters into the dumps of what has been called 'export-led retardation'. The unreasonable taxation further compounded the travails of the peasants by driving them deep into the fatal grip of moneylenders. People were tired of this suffocating colonial nexus.

As concerns began to be voiced, the British realised the imperative need to police the Indian press. The Vernacular Press Act was introduced by Lord Lytton in 1878, imposing throttling limitations on the freedom of the Indian press.

The same year, the Indian Arms Act made it a criminal offence (punishable by imprisonment and/or fine) to carry or keep arms without a licence. What made the Act doubly repressive was the show of blatant discrimination in exempting Europeans, Anglo-Indians and select categories of government officials from its purview. In 1883 the Ilbert

Bill, allowing Indian magistrates to try Europeans, was introduced. Like a flash in the pan, it was quickly withdrawn in the face of vocal British protest. British promises were proving to be hollow. With most well-paid jobs still reserved for the British, Indians faced growing unemployment. This racial discrimination, along with several other factors, spurred Indian nationalists into organising themselves into groups to get their demands accepted.

The second half of the 19th century was in many ways India's age of introspection. It was also a period of cultural renaissance. People such as Swami Vivekananda, Lokmanya Bal Gangadhar Tilak, Bipin Chandra Pal and Aurobindo Ghose began to unfold the beauties of India's rich traditions and beliefs. At the 1893 Parliament of Religions held at Chicago, India was represented by Swami Vivekananda who introduced western audiences to the catholicity of Indian culture and Hindu religion. Like Aurobindo Ghose after him, Swami Vivekananda had intense faith in the spiritual mission of India but felt that it could not be realised without getting political freedom. Bipin Chandra Pal appealed in the name of Kali and Durga for acquiring strength and cultivating the capacity to strike.

Sri Aurobindo observed, "Independence is the goal of life and Hinduism alone will fulfil this aspiration of ours." Most of the early leaders of the Extremists were under the influence of the religious revivalism that was taking place. Some of them were deeply religious individuals themselves.

Nature also joined in by playing a heavy hand in whipping up discontent against the British. The decades that followed the change of power at the imperial helm witnessed several droughts and famines that ravaged the lives of the average Indian, particularly the peasantry. Millions perished in the 1861 famine in the North West, the 1866 famine in Bengal and Orissa, the 1869 famine in Rajasthan, the 1874 famine in Bihar and the great famine of 1897 that affected about 20 million people and almost 70,000 square miles of Indian territory.

The unsympathetic attitude of the government and the highly irresponsible efforts made by it to control the situation fuelled the fury of Indians who rightly felt that any national government under similar circumstances would have staked everything to save them from the clutches of drought and hunger. The government became a target of attack. The resentment was compounded by the simultaneous outbreak of virulent bubonic plague in the western part of the Bombay Presidency.

Though the government was earnest in checking the epidemic, its strategy of requisitioning soldiers for inspecting houses and removing infected persons to isolation hospitals proved extremely unpopular. People objected to the entry of soldiers into their houses and the officers controlling the disinfection and evacuation programme became objects of hatred.

Amidst this cauldron of events, a man who openly professed to a poor opinion of Indian character and believed that Indians were unfit for higher services (which should therefore continue to be manned by the Europeans alone) was appointed as the Viceroy of India in 1898. This man was Lord George Nathaniel Curzon, a man who seldom paid any heed to popular Indian sentiments and demands, a man who was to hold the reins of British Indian administration for the next seven years ... years in which he did not hesitate to make racially demeaning statements. Even in the last year of his tenure, while delivering the convocation address at the Calcutta University in February 1905, he said:

> The higher ideal of truth, to a large extent, is a Western conception and truth took a higher place in the moral codes of the West before it had been similarly honoured in the East, where craftiness and diplomatic vile have been held in high esteem.

Viceroy Lord Curzon, who partitioned Bengal in 1905

These seven years were destined to witness many unpopular measures, including the Calcutta Corporation Act of 1899, the Indian Universities Act of 1904, but the act that earned Lord Curzon the wrath of Indians was effected on 16 October 1905. This was the socially, emotionally, religiously and nationally divisive partitioning of Bengal into two parts: Bengal and Eastern Bengal and Assam.

Even today, it remains one of Indian history's most controversial and debated acts. Proposals for partitioning Bengal were first considered in 1903. Putting forth the resolution, Sir Herbert Hope Risley (then Home

Secretary to the Indian Government) wrote, "Bengal united is power. Bengal divided will pull several different ways—one of our main objects is to split up and thereby weaken a solid body of opponents to our rule." Lord Curzon's original scheme may have been based on grounds of administrative efficiency but the vociferous, emotion charged protests and reactions against the original plan gave the British an inkling of

In his letter dated 9 February 1905, to Sir John Brodrick, Secretary of State for India, Lord Curzon wrote about the reconstruction of the province of Bengal and the constitution of a new province that was to be called the North-Eastern Provinces. He submitted two draft proclamations as follows:

The first of these (Draft I) relates to the constitution of the new Province. The effect of it is to convert the present Chief Commissioner-ship of Assam into a province with a Lieutenant Governor under Section 46 of the Indian Councils Act, 1861, and then to transfer the districts of Bengal specified in our former dispatch to the new Province under the provisions of Section 47 of that Act and of Section 4 of the Government of India Act, 1865. These Sections have not been recited in the Proclamation, because it is assumed that His Majesty's assent will be conveyed by a Royal Warrant in which they will be set out as was done in the case of Burma. An alternative course would be, first to join the Bengal districts to Assam under Section 3 of the Government of India Act, 1854 and then to convert Assam into a Lieutenant Governorship under the Act of 1861, but in our opinion the procedure adapted in the draft Proclamation is the more direct.

The second (Draft II) is concerned with the transfer of Bengal of the parts of the Central Province referred to in our former dispatch. The power to make this transfer is to be found in Section 4 of the Act of 1865 and perhaps also in Section 47 of the Act of 1861, but it has been the practice of late years to proceed only under the former Act, and Draft II has been framed in accordance with that practice. The Royal assent is not required under Section 5 of the Act of 1865 to transfers from Chief Commissionership to Lieutenant Governorship or to transfers which do not include whole districts, and we therefore propose, if you see no objection, to issue the Proclamation of our own authority, reciting Section 4 of the Act, as in the draft.

George Nathaniel Curzon
H.H. Kitchener
E.R. Elles
A.T. Arundel
Denzil Ibbetson
H.E. Richards
J.P. Hewett
E.N. Baker

the immense political benefits to be derived from dividing Bengal on minority-majority Hindu-Muslim lines.

Officially published in January 1904, the government's proposal to partition Bengal was appended by the expected, well-worded, administrative justification. To begin with, it contended that there was a need to reduce the Government of Bengal's administrative burden and thereby ensure a more efficient administration of the outlying districts. Second, the government claimed that it desired to promote the development of backward Assam by enlarging its jurisdiction and giving it a trade outlet to the sea.

Third, it said that there was an urgent necessity to unite the scattered sections of the Oriya-speaking population under a single administration. The new 106,540 square mile province, with its capital at Dhaka, subsidiary headquarters at Chittagong and a population of 31 million people, comprising 18 million Muslims and 12 million Hindus, was to be called Eastern Bengal and Assam. This implied a cutting down to size of the original province of Bengal that would now measure only 141,580 square miles, with a population of 54 million, consisting of 42 million Hindus and nine million Muslims. The dice had been loaded. The game was about to begin.

The Government of India's final decision on the partition of Bengal was promulgated on 19 July 1905 through its Resolution No. 2491. The partition came into effect on 16 October 1905. It fuelled widespread anger and resentment against British rule in India and this was expressed in many ways—protest marches, boycott of foreign goods, a flurry of fiery nationalist writings in newspapers and revolutionary action.

Lord Curzon had unwittingly succeeded in placing India on the crossroad of organised nationalist struggle. 16 October 1905 was observed as a day of national mourning. A general *hartal* (strike) was called for. This was accompanied by extensive public agitation in Bengal. Nationalist poet Rabindranath Tagore led the people to the street, singing patriotic songs and tying *rakhi*s (the ceremonial thread of protection) on the wrists of Hindus and Muslims alike. Chants of *Bande Mataram* (Hail to the Motherland) filled the air. Kitchens were shut down in houses as people observed *arandhan* (abstinence from cooking). Millions fasted in a gritty show of solidarity. And in a symbolic gesture celebrating the unbreakable unity of Bengal, protesters walked barefoot to the Ganga for a dip in the waters of the holy river that had cradled the great culture of this country.

Nationalist poet Rabindranath Tagore

The division of Bengal was termed as a 'Denigration of Mother India' by the Bengali intelligentsia (the *bhadralok*) and they vowed that they would not tolerate it. Thus, though the partition was aimed at driving a wedge between the Hindus and the Muslims, it also played a major role in creating a sense of nationhood among Indians. From the streets to the palaces, almost all sections of society expressed their anger at the

Text of the resolution sent by the Maharajas of the Princely States:

This meeting desires to record its respectful but firm protest against the proposals of the government for the partition of Bengal on the following, among other grounds:

- That these proposals are viewed with grave and widespread alarm by the people of this province and have given rise to an agitation unparalleled in its history. An opposition, so strong and so universal, should not be ignored.
- That the division of the Bengalee nation into two separate units and the disruption of its historical, social and linguistic ties would seriously interfere with the intellectual, social and material progress of the people, which it has always been a part of the traditional policy of the British Government in India to foster and to estimate.
- That the districts proposed to be separated from Bengal proper would lose several constitutional, educational and other privileges, which they have so long enjoyed.
- That this meeting is of opinion, that the wider scheme of partition, referred to by His Excellency the Viceroy, does not commend itself to public opinion, and is viewed by the people of this province with great concern and anxiety for the reason among others that its cost, initial and permanent, would seriously add to the heavy burdens already imposed on the people. Instead of allaying the anxiety and alarm which Mr. Risley's proposals had caused, it has intensified them.
- That this meeting is of the opinion that no case has been made out for the proposed measure, but that if in the opinion of the Government of India the relief of the Bengal Government is necessary, the remedy lies not in a redistribution of territorial jurisdiction, but in organic changes in the form of government, such as the conversion of the Lieutenant Governorship of Bengal into a governorship with an Executive Council like that of Bombay and Madras, and this meeting prays that the government may be pleased to withdraw the proposed measure, or adopt the remedy above suggested.
- That a copy of the foregoing resolutions under the signature of the Chairman of this meeting is to be submitted to the Government of

India and that the following gentlemen do form themselves into a committee to settle the draft memorial submitted to the meeting, watch the progress of this question and take such measures from time to time as they may be deemed fit, with a view to carry out the objects and intentions of this meeting.

Committee Members

Maharaja Sir Rameshwar Singh (K.C.I.E.) of Durbhanga, Maharaja Bahadur Sir Jateendra Mohan Tagore (K.C.I.S.), Maharaja Surya Kanta Acharya Bahadur of Mymensingh, Maharaja Jagadindra Nath Ray Bahadur of Nattore, Maharaja Manindra Chandra Nandy Bahadur, Maharaja Girija Nath Ray Bahadur, Raja Mahim Ranjan Ray Chowdhury, Raja Pramatha Bhusan Deb Ray, Raja Asutosh Nath Ray, Raja Peary Mohan Mukerjee (C.S.I.), Raja Pramada Nath Ray, Nawab Syed Amir Hosein (C.I.E.), Nawab Syed Abdus Sobhan, Raja Bahadur Shashi Shekharreswar Ray, Raja Srinath Ray, Kumar Manmatha Nath Ray Chawdhuri, Kumar Pramatha Nath Ray Chawdhuri, Kumar Manmatha Nath Mitra, Kumar Upendra Chandra Chaudhuri, Babu Dharani Kanta Lahiri Chaudhuri, Jagat Kishor Acharja Chaudhuri, Babu Gopal Das Chaudhuri, Babu Kishori Lal Goswami, Mr. N.N. Ghose, Mr. A. Chaudhuri, Mr. B.L. Chaudhuri, Mr. J. Ghosal, Mr. Satyendra Nath Tagore, Mr. A.M. Bose, Rai Bahadur Sitanath Ray, Babu Muralidhar Ray, Babu Ambika Charan Majumdar (Faridpur), Babu Charu Chandra Mullick, Babu Dwarkanath Chakravarti, Babu Surendra Nath Banerjee, Babu Narendra Nath Sen, Babu Mati Lal Ghose, Babu Girdhari Lal Ray, Seth Dooly Chand, Hon'ble Babu Bhupendra Nath Bose, Ray Bhadur Raj Kumar Sarvadhikari, Ray Prabati Sankar Chaudhuri, Raya Jatindra Nath Chaudhuri, Babu Harendra Lal Ray, Babu Anand Chandra Ray (Dacca), Babu Basanta Kumar Bose, Moulvi Mahammad Yusoff Khan Bahadur, Babu Pasupathi Nath Bose, Babu Manick Lal Seal, Maulvi Shamsul Huda, Babu Janki Nath Ray, Mr. Lal Mohan Ghose, Babu Nalin Bihari Sarkar (C.I.E.), Babu Jogendra Chandra Ghose, Kumar Dakhineswar Malia, Rai Hari Ram Goenka Bahadur, Babu Radha Charan Pal, Babu Anath Bundhu Guha (Mymensingh), Babu Raghu Nath Das, Babu Baikunta Nath Sen, Babu Harendra Nath Datta, Maharaja Kumar Prodyot Commar Tagore.

Maharaja Kumar Prodyot Commar Tagore, Member and Secretary, signed the resolution and sent it to the government.

decision. The Maharajas of the Princely States of India also came together to condemn the decision and passed a resolution asking for the dissolution of the division of Bengal.

Talking of the partition, a popular poem of the time says:

Dadabhai Naoroji (1825-1917), Indian political leader

> The weak and feeble do not have any role in the movement, because it is this weakness which has led to subjugation and bondage. The partition has awakened the people from deep slumber. Even cowherds will now sing songs of national zeal, leading to awareness among the masses. This great change is important because it has made the people of India realise the real nature of British rule. Even kings and emperors are incomparable when measured against those who fight and sacrifice their lives for the freedom of their motherland. Is there anyone who does not think about the motherland? No matter how far you travel from your shores, the attachment to the motherland remains. Even in the face of royalty, title, wealth and status, it is the ardent fervour of nationalism that takes the lion's share. The dream of freeing the country from the heartbreaking shackles of dominance by another is stronger and more pronounced. Freedom, so magnificent, cannot be compromised or bartered for any materialistic gain!

The vociferous protests against the partition of Bengal soon steamrolled into the call to embrace all that was *swadeshi* or intrinsically Indian. This was fervently accompanied by the call to boycott all that was perceived to be British—goods, services, schools, colleges, institutions, courts, administration, ideas, customs and conventions. As the strategy began to take the nation in its sweep, *swadeshi* and boycott became the twin cradles of a resurgent new Indian nationalism. At the Calcutta session of the Congress in December 1906, Dadabhai Naoroji declared *swaraj* (home rule) as the nationalist goal and the demand for *swaraj* soon became the life breath of the movement. At the same session, the Congress also passed a resolution supporting boycott and *swadeshi*. In a stirring speech, Bipin Chandra Pal said:

> You will have observed the word 'boycott' is attached to the word 'movement'. It means that it shall move, move from point to point, move from city to city, move from division to division, move from province to province till we realise the highest destiny of our people as a nation in the comity of nations. I mean *swaraj*.

The echoes were taken up far and wide. The message of *swadeshi* and boycott travelled from province to province, as predicted by Bipin

Bipin Chandra Pal (1858-1932), nationalist leader and founder of the Bande Mataram

Chandra Pal. The British watched with concern as the decision to divide Bengal seemed to slip out of their control and give birth to a new age in the history of Indian nationalism—an age that breathed fire. Their fears were well founded.

At the vortex of this fiery whirlpool of events stood the youth of Bengal. They responded with great gusto to the call of nationalism. School and college students led en masse boycotts of government-controlled institutions. As usual, the government came down with a heavy hand.

On 10 October 1905, R.W. Carlyle, the officiating Chief Secretary to the Government of Bengal, sent what came to be known as 'the Carlyle Circular' to all magistrates and collectors, directing them to warn the heads of schools and colleges whose students participated in political agitation, boycotts or picketing that their grant-in-aid and scholarship facilities would be withdrawn and that the university would also disaffiliate such institutions.

The move was protested by students and teachers alike. Motivated by the British challenge, the national leaders conceptualised a scheme of national education. Advocating the establishment of national colleges independent of government control, the National Council of Education was set up in Bengal in 1906 under the stewardship of Guroodas Banerjee 'to impart education, literary and scientific as well as technical and professional, on national lines and exclusively under national control'. The Bengal National College was established in Calcutta with Sri Aurobindo Ghose as its first Principal. Many national schools sprang up in both parts of Bengal. In Madras, the Pachaiyappa National College was expanded.

Excerpts from the Fortnightly Report of Mr. E.A. Gait, Esq., CIE, Chief Secretary to the Government of Bengal

- The Collector of Customs reports that there are unusually heavy stocks of piece goods in Calcutta, but that a worse state of congestion has been known in years previous to the commencement of the boycott movement. The congestion is attributed to heavy shipments coupled with the prospects of scarcity and the high prices of food grains. Considerable stocks of Java sugar also have accumulated owing to the recent heavy shipments. Sugar is going freely to Eastern Bengal, and, although sales have fallen recently, this is attributed not to the boycott, but to the prospects of famine and to the fact that large purchases were made before and during the *Poojas*. Indenting firms have done good business in Eastern Bengal in general goods, and the tendency seems to be to accept articles of foreign manufacture provided they have Indian mottos or inscriptions upon them.

- The collector of customs hears that more or less determined efforts are being made to enforce the boycott. It is said that Bengali priests are now refusing to conduct marriages, unless the parties take the *swadeshi* vow and wear country-made clothes. The support of the priests may give the boycott a new stimulus.
- It has been reported from Bankura that certain cloth dealers' shops have been attacked and the English-made cloth burnt. The cases are being enquired into.
- It is reported that Liverpool salt is somewhat neglected and that dealers are giving preference to Spanish salt which is sold as *swadeshi*. A large quantity of plants for biscuit-making and match-making have been imported by Bengalis during the past month.

The DAV movement also made considerable headway in Punjab. All through this course of events, youngsters kept responding to the call of their soul by enlisting themselves in extremist activities. *Swadeshi*, boycott, *Bande Mataram, swaraj* ... all four became almost synonymous watchwords for the fighters of India's freedom. The Indian media, especially the Bengali press, had opposed the partition from the very beginning. Opposition had also been voiced in some sections of the British and Anglo-Indian press, public anger against the British Government was expressed in *Jugantar, Bande Mataram* and *Sandhya*. As a result, the nationalist print media and the people associated with it faced censure and prosecution for disseminating dissent against the British Government.

Bhupendra Nath Dutt, Swami Vivekananda's brother, published an article in his newspaper that was considered seditious by the British. As per Section 124A of the Indian Penal Code, the following charge was framed against him for disseminating anger against the British:

> You, Bhupendra Nath Dutt, on the 16th day of June 1907 at Calcutta, attempted to excite disaffection towards the government established by law in British India and bring that government into hatred or contempt by printing and publishing in the *Jugantar* newspaper at Calcutta aforesaid a seditious article headed 'Dispelling of Fear,' a true translation of which is as follows:

Bhupendra Nath Dutt (Swami Vivekananda's brother) was sentenced to rigorous imprisonment by Douglas Kingsford for his 'seditious' writings

Dispelling of Fear

In the course of conversation a respected Pandit said the other day that this vast British empire was a huge sham, that it was a house without a foundation or a garland striving without a thread, that though it glittered so and looked so nice with its crimson hue, a slight pull or a little push would bring it down in fragments. But that it does not fall is due simply to our foolishness. The tide of oppression has passed over us for century after century. Subjection for a thousand years has so bewildered us with fear that we cannot muster enough courage to come out of the privacy of our houses; in order to see who is sitting today in the guise of a king on the vacant throne. We see the high diadem from a distance and begin to utter our prayers and take the name of god. Our king too, seeing the opportunity, is aggravating our internal confusion by sometimes wielding the sceptre and sometimes smiling a forced smile. He and we have never become intimately acquainted with each other.

A close look at the face of a ghost dispels all fear of it. After looking at it from a distance for so long, we too have at least come to suspect that the hands and feet of the ghost are not really so strong as its face is hideous, that the bugaboo is not really just so large as we have supposed it to be. What we ought to do now most of all therefore is to give a little push to the bugaboo and see what happens. In the Punjab, scarcely was the bugbear touched with a finger when it leapt and jumped mostly from fear and partly also from anger.

What we want now is a number of men who will take the lead in giving a poke and thus embolden the masses and infuse hope in the minds of those who are almost dead with the fear and dread. It will not do to form a combination with those who are stiff with fear. Mere words will not convince such men. They must be shown by the deeds done before their eyes that the work is not impossible exactly to the extent that they think it to be, and that the arms of the English are not so long as to grasp India and keep it within their grasp against our wish. What is wanted therefore is a number of workers who will renounce every worldly thing and break off every tie and plunge into the sea of duty; who will understand everything and then make others understand; who will die themselves and deliver others from the fear of death; who will have neither home nor son nor wife but will have only their mother, the country of their mother, the country of their birth, green with crops and well watered. Will there not be found one in the whole of Bengal, who is ready to respond to the Mother's call?

Once fear is dispelled, the path of success will be made smooth and the brag of the English will be of no avail. To remove our slavery depends on us alone. People ask how long will it take yet? Whether there is a delay or not depends on ourselves. No one else will come and widen out the path of our work. It is we ourselves who must make our own path, it is we ourselves who must carry out our ideal. Sitting idle will not advance our work. It is useless also to deceive oneself with the thought 'Time will achieve everything.' Because it is man's work which is the measure of time. A ready will and exertion can achieve in a day what cannot be accomplished in a hundred years if one lies inert like a dead body. We are labouring under the misconception that while we remain as mere lookers-on, our country will by itself shake itself free. It is we who constitute the country; our freedom is the country's freedom and the seed of our subjection lies in our own inertness. It is we ourselves who must destroy that inertness by addressing ourselves to work. It won't do to say, 'Let others do the work' and to think that we shall fully discharge our duty by merely looking on and applauding those who do the work. Everyone must taste a little more or less of death. There is no other way to life. Everybody must pay some price for independence or he will not be entitled to enjoy it. What is wanted is courage and sacrifice, and above all, a keen desire.

But now the motive for work will not come so long as subjection does not appear intolerable; so long as a burning sensation as of a fire will not be caused in our souls. So long shall we ask from our privacy—how long will it take? How long will it take? On the day on which I shall become convinced that it is my work, I shall not

যুগান্তর।

The voice of the revolutionaries: the front page of Jugantar, *dated 10 February 1907*

> run about to ask any question of anybody. It is my country and I shall keep it. By dying for the independence of my country, I shall soothe the pang in my soul. There is nothing to ask anybody else anything in this connection. I have not even the right to ask whether I shall succeed or not.

Douglas Kingsford, the Calcutta Presidency Magistrate, for whom the bomb was intended

The charge concluded: "...and thereby you, the said Bhupendra Nath Dutt, committed an offence punishable under Section 124A of the Indian Penal Code."

The notoriously harsh Douglas Kingsford, the Calcutta Presidency Magistrate, convicted the publisher, confiscated the press and sentenced Bhupendra Nath Dutt to a year's rigorous imprisonment. But the fear of prosecution could not prevent the nationalists from continuing to publish articles that they felt could be eye-openers for the masses.

Another sharply worded article that appeared in *Bande Mataram* around the same time was titled '*Lathi*s [Sticks] as a Remedy'.

From '*Lathi*s as a Remedy' (published in *Bande Mataram*)

The *Ferringhee* newspaper *The Empire* is extremely sorry that the people of the country are so ungrateful as not to express the least thankfulness or loyalty to that incarnation of kindness, the Viceroy, for his vote of the Punjab Colonisation Act. But the 'Empire' is mistaken. Perhaps the fullness of the people's heart made their words stick in their throat, and there was plenty of cause to make their hearts full. In Bengal, we have cried ourselves hoarse during the last two years, and sent up the price of paper in the market by using up quires after quires of paper for submitting petitions couched in the most correct and elegant language. But as the result of all this, we have been fortunate enough to get nothing but thrusts of *lathi*s and partitioned Bengal remains parted, but in the Punjab a hue and cry was raised as the water rate was enhanced.

The period for making the representations and submitting petitions did not last more than two weeks. The people then applied the remedy which is always applied to fools. There were a few broken heads and few houses were burnt down and the authorities gave up the idea of enhancing the water rate. The colonisation act too, became imperative. How wonderful ... Kabuli medicine is indeed the best medicine.

Newspapers that printed articles that the British considered to be seditious continued to be prosecuted by the government. On 7 June 1907, the Chief Secretary to the Government of Bengal wrote a strongly worded letter from Darjeeling to the editor of *Jugantar*. It said:

> The Lieutenant Governor has had under consideration certain articles in recent issues of your paper, the language of which is a direct incitement to violence and breach of peace. The publication of such articles is against the public interest and can't be tolerated and it is essential that it should put a stop to it. Before taking action to enforce the law, his Honour considers it right that you should first be warned such language can't be allowed. I am, therefore, to invite your attention to the orders of the Government of India.

A series of articles was published in the columns of *Bande Mataram,* exhorting Indians to realise their duty to their motherland and rise to the call of freedom. *Bande Mataram's* writings flowed from the pen of its 'editor' Aurobindo Ghose—a name that the British knew to be on the forefront of the *swadeshi* and boycott movement and also suspected as being closely linked to the emergence of youth-driven, militant nationalism in Bengal.

Charges of inciting sedition against the government were drawn up against Aurobindo Ghose (alleged by the prosecution to be the editor

Extracts from 'Politics for Indians' (published in *Bande Mataram*)

Long ago I heard a European gentleman, a veritable Anglo-Indian, say that no true Englishman would be sorry if India governs herself.

Today Mr. Morley resolves that the English rule 'must continue' perhaps forever and no doubt in this autocratic form. The idea is to keep all the machineries of government within the control of the officials of the ruling race, to work them by a majority of Englishmen so that it would not be possible to overthrow any of them by a combination. Mr. Morley has said that we cannot work the machinery of our government for a week if England generously walks out of our country. While this supposition is not conceivable in the nature of man, did it not strike Mr. Morley that if, instead of walking out, the English were by force driven out of India, the government will go on, perhaps better than before for the simple reason that the exercise of power and organisation necessary to drive out so organised an enemy will, in the struggle that would ensue, teach us to arrange our own affairs sufficiently well.

REG. NO. C. 411
SWADESHI PAPER of INDIA
TOWN 2 PICE

Bande Mataram.

A Daily Organ of Indian Nationalism.

REG. NO. C. 411
'OUR POLICY' INDIA for INDIANS
TOWN 2 PICE

VOL. II.

CALCUTTA, THURSDAY, JUNE 11, 1908.

ORIENTAL MATCH

THE ORIENT

THE TIME COMES

TEA TESTING

SELECTION.

Liberty of Thought and action.

The 11 June 1908 issue of Bande Mataram, *the* swadeshi *paper of India, featuring Swami Vivekananda's inspiring message titled 'Liberty of Thought and Action'*

of the paper), Hemendro Nath Bagchi (the newspaper's 'manager') and Apurbo Krisha Bose, (the newspaper's 'printer') under Section 124A of the Indian Penal Code for the publication of an article titled 'Politics for Indians' that appeared in the town edition of 27 June and the edition of 28 June, and the re-publication on 26 July of certain seditious articles that originally appeared in *Jugantar* newspaper.

The Defence contended that Aurobindo Ghose was not the editor but was employed as a member of the staff and his sole duty was to supply contributions to the editorial columns of the paper.

The prosecution argued strongly that Aurobindo Ghose, whether editor or not, was closely identified with the publication of *Bande Mataram*.

It said that there was evidence that Aurobindo Ghose was a shareholder in the paper and that he took the chair at a preliminary meeting held in October, the minutes of which showed that he and Bipin Chandra Pal were appointed as joint editors and that a notice was printed in the issue of the paper on 12 December to the effect that Aurobindo Ghose was the editor.

It also mentioned that this was followed on 17 December by a notice announcing that Bipin Chandra Pal had terminated his connection with the paper. It contended that Aurobindo Ghose was in Calcutta from April to July 1907 and was attending the *Bande Mataram* office and that his name was entered at the head of the list of editorial staff in the pay register for January, February and March 1907 and the entries had been subsequently erased.

The prosecution also drew on the evidence of Anukul Chandra Mukherjee, a proof-reader of *Bande Mataram,* who confessed that he had seen Aurobindo Ghose in office.

In the thick of action once again, Douglas Kingsford, Chief Presidency Magistrate, delivered the following judgement:

> ... the inference I draw is that the evidence is inconclusive. I find in it nothing, which is materially inconsistent with the theory that Aurobindo is a mere member of the editorial staff and that he is without responsibility for and without cognisance of the articles charged. I therefore acquit him.

Hemendro Nath Bagchi was also acquitted but Apurbo Krishna Bose was convicted. Delivering the judgement, Kingsford said:

> There is no evidence before me to indicate that the *Bande Mataram* habitually publishes seditious matter, and I must therefore assume that the articles charged form an exception to its general tone. I must also differentiate this case from the second *Jugantar* prosecution. Apurba is a printer and nothing more, whereas the evidence in the *Jugantar* case indicated that there was no editorial staff and that the accused combined the dual functions of editor and printer. Under the circumstances I think it is proper to pass a lenient sentence upon Apurba, and accordingly I direct that he be rigorously imprisoned for three months.

As the call of freedom echoed in the hearts of Indians, the nationalist press became vocal, beyond the country's borders, too. In the January-February 1907 issue of *Circular of Freedom*, published from California, its editor Ram Nath Puri wrote a moving article titled 'You Can Be Free:'

> We are no longer immersed in Asiatic ignorance. We no longer believe in Asiatic superstitions. The king is no longer to us the representative of God in the country. We have come to know that

> the people possess the right of appointing and dethroning kings and that they are the servants of the people. When the laws made by the people are entrusted (to be put into effect) to a person, he becomes the ruler of the people, a president or a king. The (real) king of the country is the body of laws. Take these laws from his hands, and he is no longer a king, but becomes again a subject (a citizen). Do not obey the laws made by him and he would crumble into dust.
>
> We ruled our country before the advent of the British. Selfish and deceitful policies, superstitions and religious leaders made us subject to a foreign race. We ruled our country before the advent of the British, and now we do not care that we are slaves. We were respected, and now we suffer disgrace everywhere. We are glad that we have come to our senses and an axe had been laid at the root of the foolish teaching of our ignorant leaders, the Brahmans. The task is very difficult, but the axe is sharp and works rapidly and as long as it does not accomplish its work, the British Government will continue in India.
>
> We allowed a handful of Englishmen to enter our country, we thought them to be our rulers, but we shall turn this handful of Englishmen from our country. We were free, some of us are free and we shall all of us become free. This is our human right ... even God cannot deprive us of it. No one can prevent you from pondering over these questions, but you will experience some difficulty in spreading these thoughts. But free minds care little for bodily pain. They are not afraid of fines, flogging, imprisonment, being flogged and quartered alive … .
>
> Remember the words of the poet:
>
> *Stone walls do not a prison make, nor iron bars a cage …*
>
> A free mind, which is bent on attaining human rights cannot be crushed by imprisonment, stone walls, iron bars or dark cells. Have hope. Be free in mind even if the body may be in pain.

The new militant spirit that was reflected in the columns of the nationalist newspapers and resulted in the dissemination of revolutionary ideas saw the flowering of revolutionary outfits in Bengal. The *Carlyle Circular*, aimed at crushing student participation in the *swadeshi* and boycott movements, found response in the setting up of a militant organisation of students called the Anti-Circular Society. The Anushilan Samiti, established by Pramatha Nath Mitra at the turn of the century, had already been functioning under the guise of a fitness club. From its core, in 1906, emerged Jugantar—a loosely structured, volatile federation of revolutionary groups. The Dhaka Anushilan Samiti was also launched in the same year by Pulin Bihari Das. Repression continued to

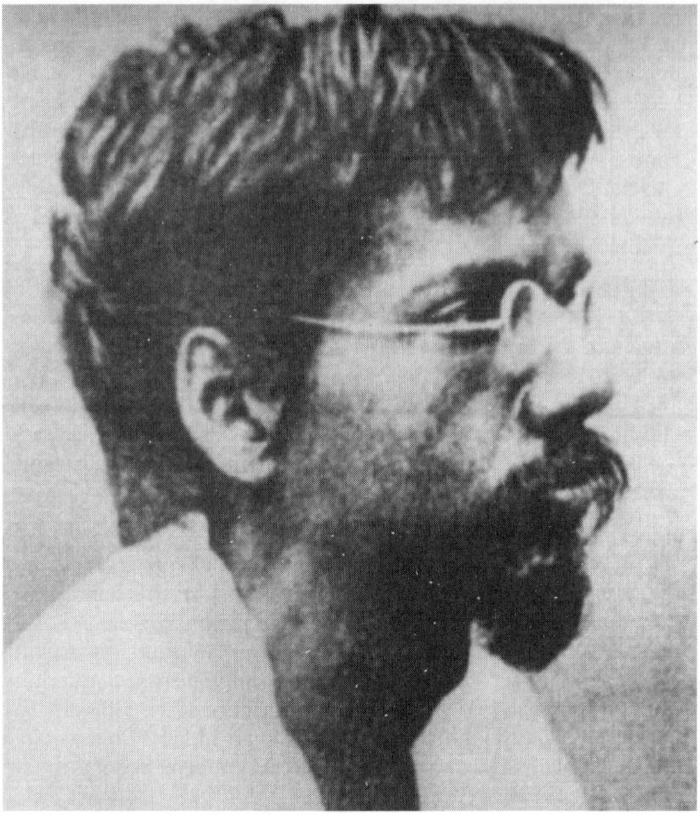

Barindra Ghose, brother of Aurobindo Ghose, used the family home as a school for revolutionaries

fuel the formation of revolutionary outfits, and soon the trend spilled over to other parts of India, especially Maharashtra, the United Provinces and the Punjab.

Like many other emotionally charged agitations, the anti-partition agitation was also initially peaceful. But as it became clear that the desired results would not be forthcoming, the reins passed into the hands of leaders who believed that a combination of boycott and terrorism could make their mission successful. Magnetised by the fiery urge to fight for their motherland, the younger generation picked up pistols and bombs. Of course, with this the anti-partition movement also entered a phase marked by violence and gradual disorder.

Less than a decade ago, British Viceroy Lord Elgin had said, "India was conquered by the sword and by the sword it shall be held!" Now, in an ironical turn of events, the youth of Bengal seemed to be returning Elgin's

A 'Book Bomb' for Kingsford

Hem Chandra Das went to France in July 1906 and is believed to have learnt bomb mechanism from Nicholas Safranski, a Russian anarchist. He returned to India in December 1907 and brought a bomb manual with him. During the investigation of the Alipore Conspiracy Case, one of the accused persons disclosed that Hem Chandra Das had prepared a book bomb that had been sent to the Calcutta residence of Mr. Kingsford in January 1908 (before he was transferred to Muzzafarpur).

The police wrote to Kingsford about this disclosure. After a few days, Kingsford wired that the article in question had been found. He recollected that the book had been handed over to his orderly in Calcutta for delivery to him (post-Independence reminiscences of the revolutionaries indicate that Paresh Moulick of Rangpur had delivered the book bomb to the orderly after Sushil Sen's initial enquiries regarding Kingsford's location and presence).

The bomb had been placed in a 1,075- page 'book' titled *A Commentary on the Common Law Designed as Introductory to its Study* by Herbert Broom. As fate would have it, Kingsford, believing it to be a book on medical jurisprudence sent to him by an IMS officer, had put it away without unfastening the tapes with which it was bound. Major Muspratt Williams, the Chief Inspector of Explosives, went to Muzaffarpur to bring the book bomb to Calcutta on 24 February 1909.

It was defused on the garden path of the residence of Mr. Frederick Loch Halliday, Commissioner of Police, Calcutta. Eighty pages at the beginning and about 400 pages at the end had been left untouched. A square had been cut out in the middle of the remaining pages in which a small Cadbury's cocoa tin containing one pound of picric acid with three detonators had been placed.

There was a spring mechanism to activate the detonators and explode the bomb on the opening of the book. The Chief Inspector of Explosives opined that had the bomb exploded, it would have proved most destructive. However, since the bomb had been lying dormant for so long, the spring and the trigger had become rusty and the compression of the spring had also gradually released.

comment. Many genuinely felt that violence was the only language the foreigners understood. Armed terrorism thus became closely intertwined with the fight for *swaraj*. In 1907, Aurobindo's brother Barindra Ghose, began using his family home in Maniktola (then a suburb of Calcutta) as an arsenal-cum-school for revolutionaries. His compatriot, Hem Chandra Das from Midnapore, went to Paris to learn bomb making and understand revolutionary politics. As Bipin Chandra Pal, Ashwini Kumar Dutta, Aurobindo Ghose and others took control of the militant movement, the police files of the British became thicker and thicker with the names of young 'suspects' and 'preventive detainees'. The same files now also had a name for this movement—'Bengal Terrorism'!

'Bengal Terrorism' was at its peak between 1908 and 1910. It was an organised movement that did not approve of individually motivated acts and secret murders. The objective was to stage a popular uprising and revolution that could bring down the edifice of British imperialism. This they hoped to do by forming secret societies that could enthuse the youth with higher values of bold action and sacrifice for the country, train them in the manufacture of bombs and explosive devices and the use of arms and also arm them for the fight.

Through the assassination of British officials they hoped to demoralise the British, paralyse the administration and uproot all enemies of India's freedom—Indians or foreigners! Guerrilla warfare, inciting the army to revolt, arranging arms supplies from nations hostile to Britain—these revolutionaries were open to following many paths.

An official report of the time mentions about 210 revolutionary outrages and 101 attempts involving hundreds of revolutionaries in the decade between 1906 and 1917 in Bengal. This includes several failed and aborted attempts on the lives of high officials between the announcement of partition in 1905 and the Muzaffarpur bombing carried out by the Jugantar revolutionaries Khudiram Bose and Prafulla Chaki in April 1908.

Chapter Two

The Retaliation

The partition of Bengal, as we have seen in the last chapter, had been promulgated in the teeth of unbridled opposition not just from the people of Bengal, but other parts of India as well. This opposition forced the Government of Bengal, the newly created Government of East Bengal and Assam and the Government of India to be on guard towards the end of Lord Curzon's tenure and especially through the entire duration of his successor, Lord Minto's stay in India from 1905 to 1910. Circulars, warnings, legislative measures and ordinances—every step was taken to abate the spread of the movement, which by 1908 had become closely allied to terrorist activities.

These were times when the Criminal Intelligence Department (CID) could hardly afford to lean back and take a moment's rest. Swamped with work, all its attention was now focused on tracing the web-like threads of revolutionary activity to their points of origin. All attempts to force a breakthrough had proved futile. On a more specific note, the CID was also aware of an assassination plot building up against the former Calcutta Presidency Chief Magistrate, Douglas Kingsford (now posted as District Judge in Muzaffarpur), but had not been able to unearth it. And then suddenly, the Muzaffarpur bombing happened!

A turning point in India's revolutionary history, the incident created a sensation in British India. The blast was followed by deafening silence in stunned British circles. Young, impassioned, 18-year-old Khudiram Bose was arrested for the bombing. Through the incident and the investigations that followed, the British were able to unravel the functioning of a well-spread network of secret societies and the people associated with it. The Muzaffarpur bombing became the starting point of the famous trial known as the Alipore Bomb Case or the Alipore Bomb Conspiracy.

The Muzaffarpur incident was the first real eruption of a volcano that had made many attempts to surface in the recent past. Before the bombing,

Khudiram Bose, who, along with Prafulla Chaki, hurled the bomb on 30 April 1908

Ullaskar Dutt, a close associate of Barindra Ghose

several unsuccessful attempts had been made on the lives of high-profile British officials. In 1906, Bampfylde Fuller, the Lieutenant Governor of the new province of Eastern Bengal and Assam, was trailed from Guwahati to Rangpur, but no attempt was made. On the night of 6 December 1907 an attempt was made near Narayangarh in the Midnapur district to blow up the train in which Andrew Fraser, the Lieutenant Governor of Bengal, was travelling. Another attempt was planned on the Lieutenant Governer's train near Chandernagore in which Barindra Ghose was accompanied by his close associate Ullaskar Dutt and Prafulla Chaki. The attempt failed because the special train did not come that way on the appointed night. December 1907 also saw a group led by Narendranath Bhattacharya carry out a dacoity in Chingripota (24 Parganas) and the shooting of B.C. Allen (District Magistrate, Dhaka) by members of the Dhaka Anushilan Samiti. On the night of 11 April 1908 an attempt had been made on the life of the Mayor of Chandernagore who had incurred the wrath of the revolutionaries for stopping a *swadeshi* meeting from taking place. The police, therefore, had enough reasons to keep a close watch on the activities of some people in Calcutta, whom they suspected of having links with the revolutionaries.

Events had been in motion for a while, but deep in their hearts the revolutionaries were getting impatient for that one big bang that could shake the British to their foundations. It is in this context that the Muzaffarpur bombing assumes great historical importance. When Khudiram Bose and Prafulla Chaki threw a bomb at what they presumed to be the carriage carrying Douglas Kingsford on 30 April 1908 in Muzaffarpur in Bihar, they brought matters to a head. Instead of assassinating Kingsford, the bomb, however, killed his bridge partners Mrs. Kennedy and Miss Grace Kennedy, the wife and daughter of Mr. Pringle Kennedy, Advocate-at-Bar at Muzaffarpur. But even though it missed the desired target, the bomb that was hurled that fateful evening blasted the myth of British invincibility and shook the empire at its roots. Indeed, even a century later, the modest bomb remains one of the loudest explosions in Indian history.

In 1908, the station club in Muzaffarpur was a lively place in the evenings. It was the leisurely hub of British officials, Europeans and the Indian elite who used to spend their time partying, relaxing and playing indoor games. Douglas Kingsford, now the District Judge of Muzaffarpur, was also a regular at the club. He had been posted away from Calcutta, but the notoriety that he had gained as Chief Presidency Magistrate and the harsh judgements that he had delivered on many nationalists had put him high on the hit list of the revolutionaries. The threat to his life had also been confirmed through a letter received by the Muzaffarpur police on 20 April 1908 from the intelligence department of the Calcutta police.

Evenings in Muzaffarpur generally wrapped up much earlier than they did in the more colourful environs of Calcutta. It was around 8.30 p.m. on Thursday, 30 April 1908. Ten days had gone by since the arrival of that letter. As the party wrapped up at the Station Club, Mrs. and Miss Kennedy left in a single-horse carriage—one that was, unfortunately, quite similar in appearance to the carriage that Douglas Kingsford used. On their way home, the ladies had to take the road that turned right or west after leaving the club grounds. The road passed in front of Kingsford's house.

It was a dark night. As the carriage reached the eastern gate of Mr. Kingsford's compound, two figures ran towards it from the opposite side (the southern side of the road), where they had been hiding under the trees. A crude handheld bomb was hurled into the carriage. The deafening blast that followed echoed for years to come. The body of the carriage was shattered and the two ladies travelling in it sustained terrible injuries. The syce, Sangat Dosadh, who had been standing on the footboard at the back of the carriage, lay senseless and wounded near the eastern gate of the Kingsford compound.

The victims were brought to Mr. Kingsford's house. Grace Kennedy died within an hour. Mrs. Kennedy's suffered much longer. She hung between life and death for more than a day, before succumbing to her injuries on the morning of Saturday, 2 May. By then, young Khudiram Bose, who, along with Prafulla Chaki, had hurled the bomb, was in the custody of the British.

The evidence given by the medical officer who examined both the ladies (before and after their death), as well as the injured syce, left no doubts that the deaths of the two ladies and the injuries received

The Bomb Used at Muzaffarpur

Only minute pieces of this bomb were recovered, and these together with the stains on the clothing of the deceased, are being analysed. It is considered unlikely that analysis will reveal the nature of the explosive used, but the bomb certainly did not contain picric acid, and was almost certainly a thin tin ball containing about six ounces of dynamite or gelignite. Its shattering effect was very small, the carriage being hardly damaged. Unfortunately it was thrown with terrible accuracy and had the assassin missed his aim by even one foot, one if not both ladies might have survived.

(Excerpt from the records)

Tell-tale evidence: A part of the powerful bomb that killed the Kennedys at Muzaffarpur on 30 April 1908

by the syce (who did not recover fully till the trial) were caused by an explosive bomb.

After the Calcutta police's tip-off on the possibility of an assassination attempt on Kingsford, two constables had been deputed to give him special protection. On 30 April, from about 6 p.m. to 7 p.m., the constables, Tehsildar Khan and Faiyazuddin, were on guard duty on the road from the gate of the station club to the eastern gate of Mr. Kingsford's compound. They saw two Bengalis on the road. Ordering them to clear out from the area, the constables escorted them beyond the east gate of the club. At 8.30 p.m. the same constables saw Mrs. Kennedy's carriage drive out of the club compound and then suddenly they heard and saw the explosion when the carriage reached the east gate of the Kingsford compound. They also saw two figures running southwards from the spot but lost sight of them in the darkness. Tehsildar Khan ran up to the carriage and, on seeing that the ladies had been seriously injured, he rushed to the police station.

The District Superintendent of Police reached the spot shortly after the blast. The constables gave a description of the two Bengalis whom they had seen earlier. Circulating the description, the District Superintendent rushed police officers by train, with directions to watch the railway station and the route from Muzaffarpur to Mokameh and Bankipur and arrest anyone who answered the description. The district administration also announced a reward of Rs. 5,000 for anyone who could apprehend the accused or assist in their arrest.

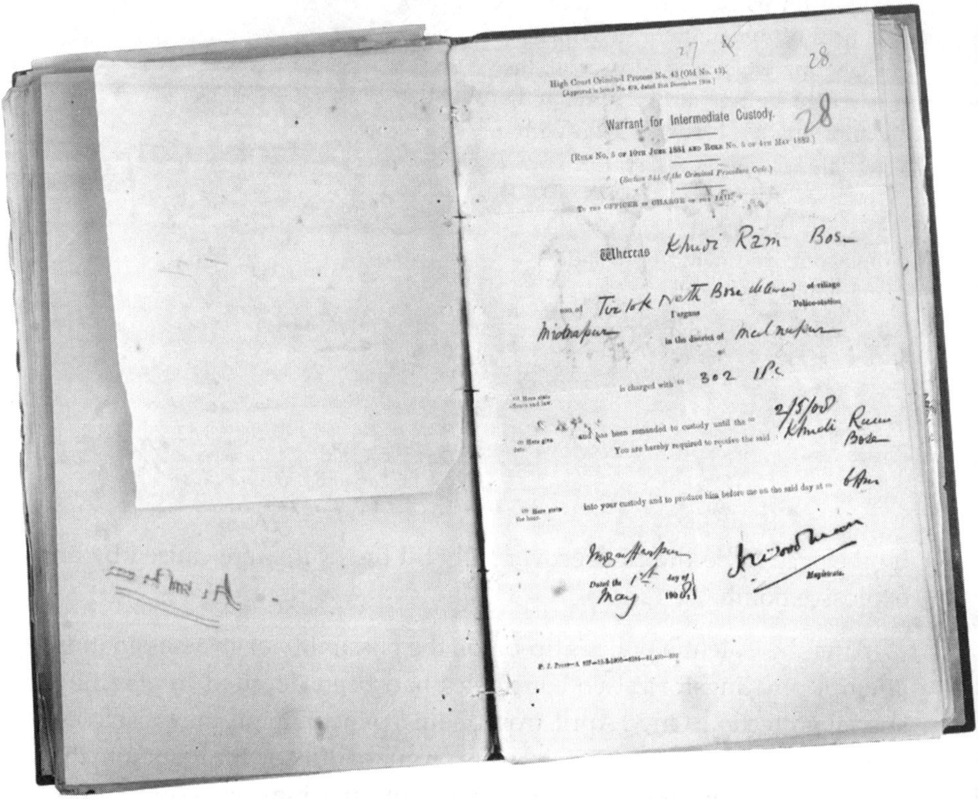

High Court Criminal Process No. 43 (Old No. 43).

Warrant for Intermediate Custody.

(Section 344 of the Criminal Procedure Code.)

To the Officer in Charge of the ...

Whereas Khudi Ram Bose

son of ... Bose ... of village ... Police-station

Midnapur in the district of Midnapur

is charged with 302 IPC

and has been remanded to custody until the 2/5/08

You are hereby required to receive the said Khudi Ram Bose

into your custody and to produce him before me on the said day at 6 am

Muzaffarpur

Dated the 1st day of May 1908

Magistrate.

The arrest warrant of Khudiram Bose, dated 1 May 1908

The next morning, at around 8 a.m., Khudiram Bose was identified by some people at a grocery shop outside Waini station (25 miles from Muzaffarpur) and arrested by constables Fateh Singh and Sheo Prasad Singh. At the time of his arrest a heavy, unloaded revolver fell out from his clothes and a small loaded revolver was snatched from him as he drew it with the apparent intention of using it. Thirty loose cartridges were also found in his pocket. A striped coat was found tied in a bundle

Khudiram Bose in the custody of policemen after his arrest

round his waist. It was later identified as the coat that he was wearing when constables Tehsildar Khan and Faiyazuddin had first accosted him outside the club compound, an hour-and-a-half before the bombing. Aside from a white silk coat none of the other articles found on his person were thought to be of any importance.

Khudiram was brought back to Muzaffarpur by the District Superintendent of Police, who had rushed to Waini on hearing of his arrest. Tehsildar Khan and Faiyazuddin identified him as one of the two men whom they had seen loitering in front of the club at about 7 p.m. on Thursday, 30 April 1908. He made a full and complete confession to the District Magistrate, accepting that he had thrown the bomb that killed the two ladies.

Giving the name of his compatriot Prafulla Chaki as Dinesh Chandra Roy, Khudiram said that he and the other man had come from Calcutta with the intention of killing Mr. Kingsford with a bomb and that they mistook Mr. Kennedy's carriage to be that of Mr. Kingsford's. Kingsford was said to have incurred the enmity of the accused and his secret society because in the discharge of his duty as Chief Presidency Magistrate in Calcutta he had convicted persons connected with certain vernacular papers for having published seditious writings. With Khudiram in custody, the hunt zeroed in on catching Prafulla.

On Friday, 1 May, at around 6 p.m., Nandlal Bannerjee, a Sub-Inspector of Police who was on leave from duty, took the train from Muzaffarpur to rejoin his station in Singbhum on the completion of his holidays. At the Samastipur station Nandlal saw a young Bengali on the platform, dressed in new clothes and shoes, whose appearance ignited his suspicion in connection with the murder at Muzaffarpur. He entered the compartment in which the young man was travelling and tried to strike up a conversation with him. This annoyed the man and he left the compartment.

At Mokameh Ghat station, Nandlal apologised and again got into the same compartment with him. In the meantime, the police officer had telegraphed his suspicions to the Muzaffarpur police and at Mokameh received a telegram directing him to arrest the young man on grounds of suspicion. The young Bengali, on hearing that he was going to be arrested in connection with the Muzaffarpur bombing incident, dashed down the platform.

The GRP (railway police) personnel on their usual duty at the station gate did not realise that the man was being chased by Sub-Inspector Nandlal Bannerjee. They heard Nandlal shout. The young boy ran towards the ladies' waiting room, where a GRP constable manning the waiting room tried to catch him. The young man then took out a pistol and fired a shot at the constables but missed. Cornered, he fired two shots at himself—one close to his collarbone and the other in his throat. Even as the twin shots rent the air, the young man collapsed and died on the spot.

The Muzaffarpur police was informed about the incident and the body was taken to Muzaffarpur for verification and investigation. On the way to Muzaffarpur, at Barauni Junction, the body was shown to constables Tehsildar Khan and Faiyazuddin who identified it as the body of the person whom they had seen loitering with the accused Khudiram Bose near the station club at Muzaffarpur.

Later, in the presence of the District Magistrate of Muzaffarpur, the body of Prafulla Chaki was shown to the accused, Khudiram Bose. Khudiram identified it as the body of his companion, naming him as 'Dinesh Chandra Roy'. The pistol with which the deceased had shot himself was also shown to the accused and though he did not recognise it, he said that Dinesh had told him that he was carrying a pistol. It has

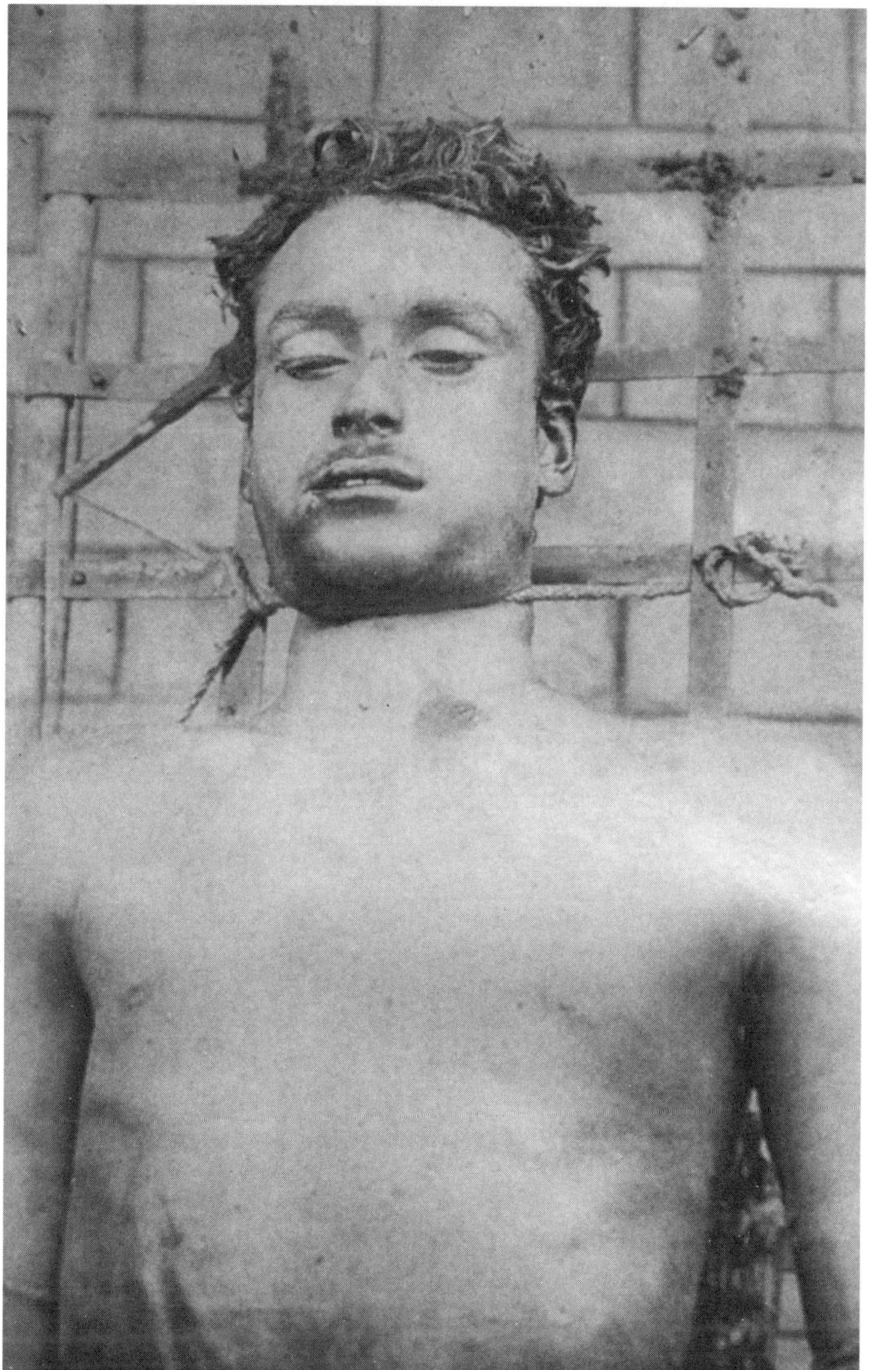

The body of Prafulla Chaki; he shot himself after hearing he would be arrested by the police

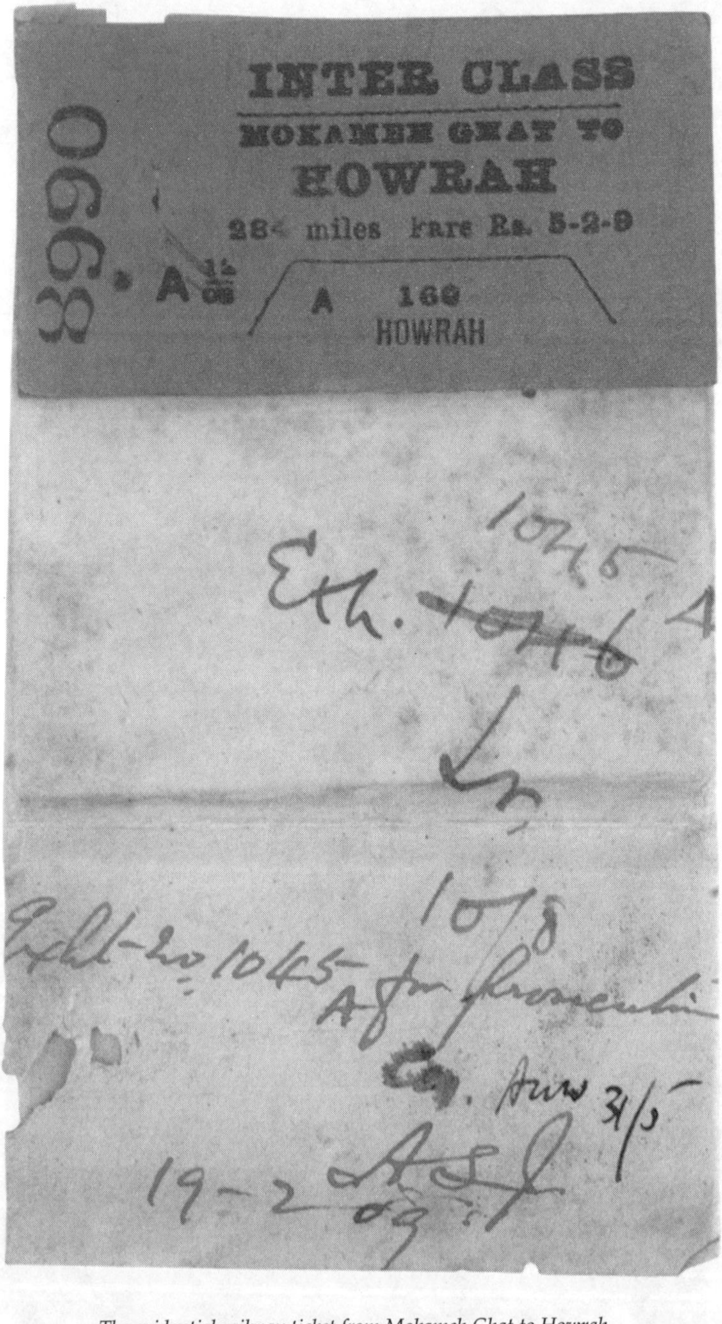

The evidential railway ticket from Mokameh Ghat to Howrah found among the possessions of Prafulla Chaki

been stated that 21 of the cartridges found with Khudiram Bose at the time of his arrest fit the pistol.

List of properties left at the scene of the incident by the accused Khudiram Bose and Dinesh Chandra Roy (deceased)*

1. Tin: 1
2. A pair of shoes belonging to the accused Khudiram Bose
3. A pair of shoes belonging to Dinesh Chandra Roy
4. A *chadar* (sheet) belonging to Dinesh Chandra Roy

List of properties found with the accused Khudiram Bose

1. Big revolver: 1
2. Small revolver: 1
3. Coat: 1
4. *Kurta reṣhmi* (silk kurta): 1
5. Bullets: 37
6. Chain and watch: 1
7. Pieces of paper, matches and a candle
8. Purse containing three currency notes of Rs. 10 each and cash Rs.1.73

List of properties found with the accused Dinesh Chandra Roy (deceased)*

1. A pair of pump shoes
2. *Punjabi* (kurta): 1
3. Revolver (Browning, with four cartridges in the magazine): 1
4. Piece of cloth: 1
5. *Endi chadar*: 1
6. *Endi chadar*: 1
7. *Banian* (vest): 1

** Dinesh Chandra Roy (Prafulla Chaki)*

Khudiram Bose had earlier been arrested in February 1906 for circulating a nationalist pamphlet. In April 1906, a sedition case had also been filed against him.

The statement of Khudiram Bose, as recorded in the 1906 sedition case

What is your name?
Khudiram Bose.

How old you are?
Fifteen years.

What is your father's name?
Trailokyanath Bose.

What caste do you belong to?
Kayastha.

What is your occupation?
I weave a loom in the weaving house of Bande Mataram Bhikshuk Sampradai.

Where is your house?
Berballabum town, Midnapur.

Will you speak of your own accord?
Yes.

Nobody has instructed you?
No.

What do you wish to say?
I went to see the mela, the day before it closed. A bearded man whom I did not know was distributing some red or green papers. He gave me six copies, I gave away two copies as I had no use for so many. The policeman saw me. He came and said, "Babu is calling you." And having said this, he started pulling me along by my hand. I said, "Leave me. I shall go of my own will." He was not leaving [me]. I gave a blow on his hand and fled away after freeing my hand from him. The form happened to fall from my hand when I was being pulled along to the constables.

Did you go to the mela on the day of the judge distributing the prize?
Yes, but I went at 10 on that day.

Did you distribute the paper on that day?
Yes.

Did you read that paper before you distributed it?
No. I read it on the next day, having got it from another boy.

Did you read that paper the day when the judge went to distribute the prizes?
No.

Will you recognise the bearded man on seeing him?
I will recognise him, if I see now.

Immediately after the murder, the District Magistrate of Muzaffarpur reached the scene of the occurrence. When he had seen to the two injured ladies in the judge's house and the wounded syce who lay beside the culvert close to the scene of the explosion, his attention had been called by a head constable to a shoe lying on the ground that lay south of the trees from under which the two attackers were said to have emerged.

Three other shoes were found afterwards in a heap of gravel on one side of the road. The three shoes included a pair that was found placed side by side, as if taken off and left there by the owner. The District Superintendent of Police also found a tin box containing a piece of cloth, lying a short distance away on the ground south of the road.

On 6 May, this pair of shoes was tried in jail on the feet of Khudiram by the Deputy Magistrate, Mr. Rowland Chandra. The shoes fit him. In fact, Khudiram is stated to have told the Deputy Magistrate that "They are my shoes." Three days earlier, on 3 May, the two shoes that were found lying apart had already been tried by the constable Mohammad Zamirul Hosain on the feet of the dead body of Prafulla Chaki. They made a perfect fit as well. Another constable, Yakub Ali, stated that on 30 April 1908 when he was returning from duty at about 8.30 p.m. he had intercepted two men—one wearing a striped coat and the other a white one—running towards the *dharamshala* (charity-run resthouse) on the road between the *dharamshala* and the charitable dispensary. On being questioned, the men had said that they were running to catch up with a friend. After the body of Dinesh Chandra Roy reached Muzaffarpur, the District Magistrate and the District Superintendent of Police took the accused Khudiram to the *dharamshala* where it is said that he showed the room in which he and Dinesh had stayed. The door to the room was locked and was hence broken open. During the search that followed, among other things, a canvas bag was found. At the bottom of the bag there was a layer of cotton wool that had two indentations. One of these seemed to have been caused by the tin box that had been picked up by the District Superintendent near the scene of the occurrence.

List of articles recovered from the *dharamshala*

1. Brass lock: 1
2. A hand bag containing cotton (taken away by the Explosives Inspector)
3. Potatoes
4. Salt

5. Flower in a plantain leaf
6. Pieces of a timetable
7. Turmeric powder
8. A piece of cloth
9. Stocking: 1
10. Towel: 1 (Dinesh)
11. A *dhoti* with a black border belonging to Khudiram Bose
12. Fuel
13. A *malmal* (muslin) *dhoti* with some rice belonging to Dinesh
14. A *dhoti* with a red border belonging to Dinesh
15. Blanket: 1 (Dinesh)
16. Piece of *chhalti* cloth
17. Burnt piece of paper and matches
18. *Handi* (earthen pot): 1
19. *Handi:* 1
20. Brass tumbler of Dinesh
21. *Nadia:* 1
22. *Katia:* 1
23. Timetable: 1

Two servants employed at the *dharamshala,* Kheman and Ramdhari Misser, stated that the accused Khudiram Bose and his companion stayed at the *dharamshala* from 10 or 11 April to the date of the bombing.

Another witness, Keshublal Chatterjee, said that he had seen the appellant on the Secunderapur *Maidan* (ground) in Muzaffarpur on 10 April and had spoken to him.

In the light of the statement of these facts and the circumstantial evidence available, the case for prosecution was that the accused Khudiram Bose and his companion Dinesh Chandra Roy/Prafulla Chaki (deceased) had been in Muzaffarpur for quite a few days prior to the bombing, waiting for an opportunity to carry out their intention of murdering Mr. Kingsford.

Twenty-four witnesses were examined to prove the above facts. The evidence of the medical officer was also submitted. The witnesses included the District Magistrate and the District Superintendent of Police who proved the discoveries made on the spot after the murder, the arrival of the accused after his arrest, his confession, his identification by the two constables and his identification by Kaliram—the coachman of Mr. Kennedy's carriage—and the discovery of the canvas bag in the room in the *dharamshala*. They also proved the arrival of the body of the other man, Dinesh Chandra Roy, his identification by the accused and Babu Jotish Chandra Sen (the Sub Divisional Officer of Barh) and the identification of the deceased by the two constables, as the man whom they had seen with the accused at 7 p.m. on the evening of the bombing.

The District Judge, Mr. Kingsford, proved that the two injured ladies were driven to his house and also the death of Miss Kennedy shortly afterwards. He also proved that he heard that an attempt was to be made on his life by somebody sent from Calcutta.

The coachman Kaliram was also questioned. It appeared that when examined by the District Magistrate immediately after the incident, he said that he had seen a man run out from under a tree and throw the bomb. The next morning—before seeing the accused—he said that there were two men who came out from under the trees, one of whom threw the bomb into the carriage. The other man, he said, also threw something that exploded and struck him in the back. This witness and another, Mr. Wilson, who was offered for cross examination, were the only ones who spoke of two explosions.

The coachman repeated his second story in court and distinctly said that he identified the appellant as the man who threw the bomb. The Sessions Judge accepted his evidence on this point. The syce, Sangat Dosadh, proved the throwing of the bomb but he spoke only of "one man who was dressed in white". He had been injured by the explosion and thrown senseless from the carriage.

The constables Tehsildar Khan and Faiyazuddin proved that they had seen the appellant and his companion loitering on the road outside the clubhouse at 7 p.m. on the night of the bombing and had ordered them to move on. Stating that they had heard and seen the explosion when the bomb was thrown, they afterwards identified the accused Khudiram Bose and the deceased Dinesh Chandra Roy.

The evidence of Colonel Graviger (I.M.S.) proved the injuries sustained by Mrs. and Miss Kennedy and that their deaths were due to those injuries. In addition, there was the confession made by Khudiram to the District Magistrate and his statement, recorded by the committing Magistrate.

Realising the importance of the case and its connection with the existence of secret societies and the struggle for India's freedom, the government decided to appoint Mr. H.W.C. Carnduff, Additional Sessions Judge, Muzaffarpur, to try the historic case. On 27 May 1908, Mr. E.A. Gait, Chief Secretary to the Government of Bengal, wrote a letter to Carnduff, informing him: "Under Section 193 (a) of the Code of Criminal Procedure, the Lieutenant Governor directs you to try the case of the King Emperor versus Khudiram Bose and Kishori Mohan Banerjee [an accused in another case] committed by E.H. Berthoud, Esq., officiating Joint Magistrate on 25 May 1908 to the Court of Session, Muzaffarpur, for trial of the former on charges under Sections 302 and 114 of the Indian Penal Code and the latter under Section 201 of that code."

Following the appointment of the judge, charges were framed against Khudiram Bose and the trial began in the court. While Babu Binode Bihari Mazumdar appeared for the Crown, Khudiram Bose was undefended (the other accused, Kishori Mohan Banerji, was defended by Babu Gobind Chunder Rai). Khudiram Bose was brought before the Court in custody and the charge of murder was read and explained to him. Stating that he understood the charge, Khudiram pleaded guilty.

The trial did not meander for long and on 13 June 1908, in the Court of the Sessions Judge, H.W.C. Carnduff, Additional Sessions Judge of Muzaffarpur, pronounced a judgement that wasn't really unexpected. In his judgement, he said:

> On the night of 30 April last, at about half-past 8, Mrs. and Miss Kennedy were returning home in the dark from the Muzaffarpur station club. While going past the judge's house a bomb was thrown in their carriage and exploded—shattering the vehicle, sustaining injuries to the syce on the footboard and causing such frightful injuries to the unfortunate ladies that the younger one of them died within an hour of the accident and the other, seriously injured, in the morning of 2 May 1908. The theory of prosecution is that the bomb was intended for Mr. Kingsford, the District and Sessions Judge of Muzaffarpur, who had shortly before been transferred from the appointment of Chief Presidency Magistrate of Calcutta. The prisoner Khudiram Bose is standing charged with the murder, and I should have no hesitation in convicting the prisoner of murder on the circumstantial evidence, therefore, and agreeing with both assessors, I hereby do so.
>
> The evidence had been discussed by the District Judge in his summing up of the case to the assessors, which summing up he asks in his judgement may be read as part of his judgement. In his judgement, he finds that the circumstantial evidence against

> the accused is overwhelming and fully established his guilt of the offence of murder and he says that he convicts the accused on that evidence. He adds that he sees no reason for doubting the voluntary character of the confession made by the accused to the District Magistrate or of the plea of guilty made by the accused to the charge. He said:
>
> The sentence of the Court is that the prisoner Khudiram Bose be hanged by the neck until he is dead.

Khudiram Bose subsequently appealed in the High Court of Calcutta against the judgement of the Sessions Judge and pleaded for the retrial of the case on various grounds. The judges of the High Court dealt with the various objections of the accused thoroughly and, giving their opinion, they said:

> The circumstantial evidence against the accused in this case is overwhelming and is in our opinion consistent only with the conclusion that the accused committed the offence with which he was charged. However improper some of the questions may have been, it is in our opinion clear that the whole examination cannot be rejected as inadmissible and it is unfortunate that owing to the method adopted by the judge of incorporating his summing up into his judgement it is not clear how much he accepted. It is evident from the proceedings before the Sessions Judge that the appellant made no effort to dispute the truth of the case for the prosecution or to deny his guilt or that he was present at the scene of the murder.
>
> The evidence for the prosecution stands practically unchallenged at the trial and in the course of this appeal, except the evidence of the coachman. As to the evidence of this witness we see no reason to differ from the conclusion of the Sessions Court that it may be accepted so far as the identification of the accused as the man who threw the bomb is concerned. His first statement taken immediately after the excitement of the occurrence when he must have been suffering from terror and excitement cannot be relied on implicitly. The second statement was made before the accused was brought in under arrest and we think that it may be accepted. As regards the identification of the accused we think we should hesitate to differ from the finding of the District Judge who had the witness before him and saw his demeanour under examination.
>
> At the time of the occurrence the lamps of the carriage were alight and it was certainly possible to see distinctly the face of a person approaching the carriage especially as the evidence to the effect is that the accused's head was uncovered.

Apart from the evidence of this witness, however, we have it proved that prior to the occurrence the accused and his companion were staying in Muzaffarpur for no ostensible object and that the accused gave a false description of himself. On the night of the occurrence the accused and his companion were seen loitering near the scene of occurrence an hour before the murder. Two men were seen to run up to the carriage when the bomb was thrown and two figures were seen running away from the scene of occurrence. Afterwards also, two men were seen running to the *dharamshala* whose description tallied with that of the accused and his companion. Two pair of shoes, one pair belonging to each of them, were found close to the scene of the murder.

After the murder, the accused and his companion fled in different directions leaving the room in the *dharamshala* locked with their things in it. The accused was arrested 25 miles off the next morning. He was armed with two revolvers and was carrying loose cartridges. He attempted to escape at the time of his arrest. Round his body were found a striped coat and a white coat similar to those which he and his companion were wearing before the occurrence. Close to the scene of occurrence was found a tin box which corresponded with the marks in the cotton wool in the bag belonging to the two men found in the *dharamshala* and which, as it had evidently been carried with care, presumably contained the bomb with which the murder was committed.

The accused's companion was arrested two days afterwards dressed in new clothes and shoes and after he had tried to escape and shoot one of his captors, he committed suicide. Some of the spare cartridges that were found with the accused fitted the pistol with which Dinesh Chandra Roy shot himself. These facts combined, make out against the accused a very strong case and are in our opinion consistent with the one view only, namely that he committed the murder as charged.

In his petition of appeal too there is no denial of his guilt or at least of his being implicated in the crime. In the first ground he says that he made his statement to the DM in order to save Dinesh Chandra Roy as he had been instructed by that person and in the remaining grounds he suggests that burdened as he was with two pistols and other articles and ignorant as he was of how to use a pistol or to throw a bomb, interests with this Court to consider whether the bomb was thrown by him or Dinesh Chandra Roy. [sic]

In the last ground he suggests that Dinesh Chandra committed suicide only because he was absolutely guilty or he threw the bomb. He and Dinesh went that night with the intention of committing murder by means of the bomb and if in prosecution of this common object the accused stood by and held the heavy articles and the coat of Dinesh so as to facilitate the commission of the offence by Dinesh and to assist his escape afterwards, and if Dinesh threw the bomb, the accused would be equally guilty with Dinesh of committing the offence of murder (Section 34 I.P.C.).

The first object of attack is the judgement of the Sessions Judge. It is urged that the judge could not under the law embody his summing up to the assessors in his judgement, that therefore the judgement was incomplete as containing no statement or discussion of the evidence and that on this ground the conviction cannot stand and that it should be set aside and a retrial ordered.

The objection in our opinion is purely technical and has no real substance. If the judge had made a copy of his summary and had included it in the judgement it is not disputed that there could be no legal objection to its being treated as a part of the judgement. Such a summary would indeed form a natural part of the judgement and though in it the facts and evidence are marshalled for the assistance of the assessors they are in reality the facts and evidence on which the determination of the case depended, the ultimate decision of which rested with the Sessions Judge.

In his judgement the judge records his findings on the facts and evidence as explained in his summary and though his method is inconvenient and not one of which we could approve for general adoption, we are unable to hold that it is illegal or that it vitiates the judgement so as to render it invalid.

The case has been tried with great care and fairness by the Sessions Judge and every assistance that was possible was given to the accused for his defence. It remains for us to determine whether there are to be found in this case any extenuating circumstances in favour of the accused which would, in law, justify us in reducing the extreme sentence which has been passed by the Sessions Judge and delaying with this question we are bound by the law and can only give effect to considerations which would in law justify us in interfering with the sentence. The learned pleader for the appellant in pleading on behalf of his client for mitigation of the sentence has urged the following facts:

1. His youth, his age being about 19 years.
2. His confession to the District Magistrate, which shows that his feelings have not been fully developed and that the crime was an insane act of criminal folly.
3. His attitude during the trial, which goes to support the inference that the accused is not a young man of a strong mind and that he was a mere tool in the hands of others.

> The accused is not a mere youth but a young man who has attended the age fixed for the majority in this country. The crime was not committed at the instigation of an older man present in the spot. For 20 days the accused and his companion had been in Muzaffarpur watching for an opportunity to commit the crime, and when they thought the opportunity offered itself they carried it out with deliberation and determination after first taking precautions to avoid detection and secure escape. It is impossible to treat the accused as a young man who did not know fully well the serious nature of crime he was committing. The murder was deliberately planned and cruelly carried out under cover of the darkness by the accused and his companion, both being armed with pistols and having made careful preparations for their own safety and escape.
>
> We can find in the case no extenuating circumstances which would in law justify our interference with the extreme sentence which has been passed on the accused by the Sessions Judge. We, therefore, confirm conviction and sentence and dismiss the appeal.

The above judgement was pronounced by Mr. C.M.W Brett and Mr. A.E. Ryves, the Judges of the High Court of Calcutta on 13 July 1908.

Khudiram Bose was hanged on 11 August 1908, hailed by the nation as a martyr who sacrificed himself for his motherland.

Chapter Three

The Trial and The Judgement

The Muzaffarpur bombing of 30 April 1908 was a rude wake-up call for the administration. It came to terms with the harsh reality that the bomb was indeed intended to kill Douglas Kingsford—something about which they already had information from the Calcutta police.

As mentioned before, for some time now and particularly since the Narayangarh train wrecking case, the police, in association with the CID of Calcutta, had been keeping vigil at various places in the city to unearth the existence of secret societies. The Muzaffarpur bombing made them tighten their surveillance and follow it up with extensive and well-planned raids at the break of dawn on 2 May 1908, to unearth more information.

The First Information Report

A First Information Report (FIR) was subsequently lodged by Babu Puran Chandra Biswas, Inspector, CID, Bengal, where it was mentioned:

> In course of the investigation of the Narayangarh train wrecking case, Midnapur, which occurred on the morning of 6 December last, a clue was obtained of the existence of a secret society working with its headquarters at various places in Calcutta. The information thus received was followed up and a number of officers detailed to watch its operations in plain clothes. The following are some of the important places where its members used to conspire together against the lives of the rulers of the country, in view of overawing the Imperial and the Provincial Governments in India by means of criminal force or shows of criminal force to secure independence of their country.
>
> 1. 32 Muraripukur Garden House, which is the joint property of Aurobindo Ghose, Barindra Ghose and their two brothers Manomohan Ghose and Benoy Ghose.
>
> 2. 23 Scott's Lane, where Aurobindo Ghose, Barindra Ghose and their friends Abinash Chandra Bhattacharji and Sailendra Bose used to mess together.

The epicentre of revolutionary activity: The Muraripukur Garden House or Bagan Bari

3. 38-4 Raja Nava Kissen Street, where explosives were prepared by accused Hem Chandra Das.

4. 15 Gopi Mohan Dutta's Lane, where some of the explosives were stored and manufactured by the members of this society.

5. 4 Harrison Road, where the Jugantar bookshop opened.

6. 30-2 Harrison Road, where the members of this society used to congregate from time-to-time in view of carrying on correspondence with its other members working or employed at other places.

7. 134 Harrison Road, where some of the explosives and ammunitions were stored.

8. Navasakti office, where Aurobindo Ghose, his brother Barindra Ghose and their friends Abinash Chandra Bhattacharji and Sailendra Bose removed to on 30 April last.

The Book of Explosives

The Book of Explosives was found in the Maniktolla garden. The general purpose was well described in its opening sentence, 'The aim of the present work is to place in the hands of a revolutionary people such a powerful weapon as explosive matter is.' Major Smallwood, the Chief Inspector of Explosives, described it as the best guide to explosives he had ever seen. It was divided into the following chapters:

1. Preparation of the Explosive Substances
2. Fabrication of Shells
3. Use of Explosives

The subject is exhaustively and apparently scientifically treated; the amount of attention given to detail may be gathered from the fact that the composition and manufacture of 30 different explosives of one class only, that is, those containing salts of chloric and chlorous acids, are described. In the second chapter, the making of percussion bombs and fuse bombs is described as well as the proper way to make an instantaneous fuse, a 15-second fuse, a three-minute fuse, up to an eight- or nine-hours fuse. A complete manual for anarchists, it was very clearly from a European source. Only one complete copy of the manual was found. It was in a manuscript. Notebooks were also found into which the manual was in the process of being copied.

On the first instance, with the information received of the outrage at Muzaffarpur necessitating immediate action, the police as well as spies acting on a tip-off and definite information made arrangements on 1 May to search various places which were under surveillance and for the purpose they obtained search warrants for simultaneous house searches in Calcutta. On 2 May at 5.00 a.m. the searches commenced at different centres and arrests were made with the results noted below:

1. At the Muraripukur Garden Centre, 18 persons were arrested. The building consisted of a large room, a small room on one end of this large room, a verandah in front and a verandah at the back running along one side of the building. The 13 accused were arrested from the front verandah and Upendra Nath Banerjee from a small room.

They are:

(1) Barindra Kumar Ghose (2) Indu Bhusan Rai of Khulna (3) Ullaskar Dutt of Tippera (4) Upendra Nath Banerjee of Chandernagore (5) Sishir Kumar Ghose of Jessore (6) Nalini Kumar

Gupta of Faridpur (7) Sachindra Kumar Sen of Dacca (8) Paresh Chandra Moulik of Jessore (9) Kunjalal Shaha of Nadia (10) Bejoy Kumar Nag of Khulna (11) Narendra Nath Bakshi of Rajshahi (12) Purna Chandra Sen of Midnapur (13) Hemendra Nath Ghose of Jessore (14) Bibhuti Bhusan Sarkar of Nadia (15) Nidhi Uria of Cuttack (16) Panu Uria of Cuttack (17) Sachindra Nath Chatterjee of Calcutta (18) Indu Bhusan Bose of Calcutta. The last four had subsequently been released on bail. Many articles were found from this place like—voluminous correspondence, explosives, guns, rifles, revolvers, dynamite and articles used in manufacture of explosives, which were buried underground and pointed out by Barindra Kumar Ghose.

2. At 38-4 Raja Navakissen Street, accused Hem Chandra Das was arrested and a quantity of incriminating correspondence was seized together with other articles.

3. At 15 Gopi Mohan Dutt's Lane, accused Kanai Lal Dutt of Hugli and Nirapada Rai of Nadia were arrested with a large quantity of correspondence and other papers.

4. At 30-2 Harrison Road, some papers were found which were taken into possession.

5. At 134 Harrison Road, Nagendra Nath Gupta of Dacca, his brother Nalini Gupta of Dacca, Ashoke Chandra Nandi of Comilla, Bejoy Sen Gupta of Burdwan and Motilal Bose of Jessore were arrested with a quantity of bombs, dynamites, cartridges and other explosives.

6. At Navasakti office, accused Aurobindo Ghose, Abinash Chandra Bhattacharji and Shalendra Kumar Bose of 24 Parganas were arrested and with them a quantity of incriminating correspondence was found.

On 3 May 1908 at No. 80, College Street, Din Dayal Bose of 24 Paraganas was arrested where letters and correspondence were found and seized.

On 5 May 1908 accused Narendra Nath Gossain of Serampur, Hugli was arrested at that place with lots of papers, cartridges, buckshot and caps.

On 10 May 1908, accused Sudhir Sarkar of Khulna and Hrishikesh Kanjilal of Hugli were arrested at their homes and some articles, papers and letters were found. The recovered articles from each place had been submitted and lists were made accordingly to produce in the Court. Of the persons thus arrested, the following had confessed:

(i) Upendra Nath Bannerjee: Accepted the existence of the secret society and his being a member of it.

(ii) Barindra Kumar Ghose: He also confessed the existence of the secret society and his involvement in it. He accepted his participation in the preparation for derailing the Governor's special train between Mankundu and Chandernagore railway stations, the Narayangarh derailment case in December 1907, the French Chandernagore bomb outrage case in April 1908 and to the abetment of the Muzaffarpur murder case on 30 April 1908.

(iii) Indu Bhusan Rai: He also confessed to the existence of the secret society and to his participation in the French Chandernagore bomb outrage case.

(iv) Bibhuti Bhusan Sarkar: Accepted the existence of the secret society and his complicity in derailing the Governor's special train between Chandernagore and Mankundu railway station and also in the Midnapur train derailing case.

(v) Ullaskar Dutt: Accepted the existence of the secret society and his involvement in derailing the Governor's special train near Chandernagore railway station, again the same in Mankundu Railway station and Narayangarh train wrecking case, French Chandernagore bomb outrage and the Muzaffarpur murder case.

From the above it will appear that altogether five cases occurred as the outcome of the conspiracy of the secret society. These are:

1. Attempt at wrecking His Honour's special train between Mankundu and Chandernagore railway stations at or about the last Diwali. Accused Ullaskar Dutt, Hrishikesh Kanjilal and Narendra Nath Gossain who took part in it are under arrest. They have all confessed to their participation in the incident.

2. Preparation for blowing up His Honour's special between Mankundu and Chandernagore railway stations during last winter. Accused Barindra Kumar Ghose, Bibhuti Bhusan Sarkar and Ullaskar Dutt who were concerned in the act have confessed to the same.

3. Attempt at wrecking His Honour's special near Narayangarh railway station in Midnapur on 6th December 1907. Accused Barindra Kumar Ghose, Bibhuti Bhusan Sarkar and Prafulla Chaki who actually laid the mine and Ullaskar Dutt who made it were under arrest. Prafulla Chaki committed suicide after the murder of Muzaffarpur.

4. The French Chandernagore bomb outrage case on 11 April 1908. The accused in the case Barindra Kumar Ghose, Narendra Nath Gossain, Indu Bhusan Rai have confessed to the involvement. The bomb used in this case was made by Hem Chandra Das and Ullaskar Dutt. Of them, the latter has confessed of it.

> 5. Muzaffarpur murder case on 30 April 1908. The bomb used in the case was made by Hem Chandra Das and Ullaskar Dutt. Ullaskar Dutt has confessed to the fact. The plot was organised by Barindra Kumar Ghose who has confessed his complicity in the incident. Of the two persons actually concerned in the murder of Mrs. and Ms. Kennedy, namely Khudiram Bose of Midnapur and Prafulla Chaki of Bogra, the former has been arrested and confessed and the latter committed suicide when an attempt of arresting him was being made.
>
> On 12 May 1908, Kristo Jiban Sanyal of Maldah and on 14 May 1908, Barindra Nath Ghose of Jessore were arrested and have confessed to being members of the secret society.
>
> In consideration of the facts already disclosed, I submit this First Information Report, charging the members of this secret society under Sections 143, 145, 150, 157, 121, 121A, 122, 123 and 124 IPC.

In order to prosecute the accused, F.W. Duke, Chief Secretary to Government of Bengal had issued a sanction order in which he stated that "There is reason to believe that during a period commencing from about 16 October 1905 to date at Manicktolla (32, Muraripukur Road), Calcutta and other places, that is, the date of arrest, the following persons have committed offences punishable under Sections 121A, 122, 123 and 124 of the Indian Penal Code.

Babu Puran Chandra Biswas, Inspector of Police, CID, Bengal, was authorised by His Honour the Lieutenant Governor of Bengal under the provision of Section 196 of the Code of Criminal Procedure to prefer complaint against and to prosecute accused persons."

Accordingly, Puran Chandra Biswas, Inspector of Police, CID Bengal, complained against:

1. Barindra Kumar Ghose, son of K.D. Ghose of 32, Muraripukur Road
2. Indu Bhusan Rai, son of Tarak Nath Rai of Sriphaltola, Khulna
3. Ullaskar Dutt, son of Dwijadas Dutt of Kalikanchha, Brahmanberia, Tippera
4. Upendra Nath Banerjee, son of Roma Nath Banerjee, of Gondalpara, French Chandernagore
5. Sishir Kumar Ghose, son of Tarini Ghose of Sagordari, Keshabpur, Jessore

6. Nalini Kumar Gupta, son of Rajani Kumar Gupta of Harowa, Faridpur
7. Sachindra Kumar Sen, son of Debendra Nath Sen of Sonarang, Munshiganj, Dacca
8. Paresh Chandra Moulik, son of Jadav Chandra Moulik of Rainagar, Magura, Jessore
9. Kunja Lall Shaha, son of Ram Lall Shaha of Mozampur, Kushtea, Nadia
10. Bejoy Kumar Nag, son of Bepin Behari Nag of Basahabati Bagerhat, Khulna
11. Narendra Nath Bakshi, son of Umesh Chandra Bakshi of Mathpur, P.S., Mohadevpur, Rajshahi
12. Purna Chandra Sen, son of Jogindra Nath Sen of Chandpur, Daspur, Midnapur
13. Hemendra Nath Ghose, son of Rai Charan Ghose of Sagordari, Kesbabpur, Jessore
14. Bibhuti Bhushan Sarkar, son of Saroda Sarkar of Sutragarh, Santipur, Nadia
15. Nirapodo Rai, son of Rajani Kanta Rai of Baghchra, Santipur, Nadia
16. Kanai Lal Dutt, son of Chuni Lal Dutt, Tantipara, Serampur, Hughli
17. Hem Chandra Das, son of Khettra Mohan Das of Radhanagore, Narayangarh, Midnapur
18. Aurobindo Ghose, son of KD Ghose of 48, Grey Street (Navasakti office)
19. Abinash Chandra Bhattacharji, son of Umacharan Bhattacharji of Arbellia, Baduria, 24 Parganas
20. Sailendra Nath Bose, son of Kedar Nath Bose of Arbellia, Baduria, 24 Parganas
21. Nogendra Nath Gupta, son of Girija Prosanna Gupta of Bidgaon, Munshiganj, Dacca
22. Dharani Nath Gupta, son of Girija Prosanna Gupta of Bidgaon, Munshiganj, Dacca

23. Asoke Chandra Nandy, son of Mohendra Chandra Nandy of Kalikanchha, Brahmanberia, Comilla
24. Bejoy Ratna Sen Gupta, son of Gopal Chandra Sen Gupta of Satgoria, Purbesthali, Burdwan,
25. Moti Lal Bose, son of Poresh Nath Bose of Simuria, Narail, Jessore
26. Din Dayal Bose, son of Kedar Nath Bose of Arbellia, Baduria, 24 Parganas
27. Narendra Nath Gossain, son of Debendra Nath Gossain of Serampur, Hooghly
28. Sudhir Kumar Sarkar, son of Prosanna Kumar Sarkar, Civil Hospital Assistant, Khulna
29. Kristo Jiban Sanyal, son of Kali Kristo Sanyal of Kansat, P.O. Kansat, Maldah
30. Hrishikesh Kanjilal, son of Amar Nath Kanjilal of Chatra Serampur, Hooghly
31. Birendra Nath Ghose, son of Trailokya Nath Ghose of Sagordari, Keshabpur, Jessore
32. Khudiram Bose (under arrest in Muzaffarpur)
33. Sushil Kumar Sen, son of Kailash Chandra Sen of Beniachang, P.S. Beniachang, Sylhet

All those named above were accused of organising a gang for the purpose of waging war against the government and overawing the government by means of criminal force. From 4 to 19 May 1908 — from time-to-time, as they were arrested — the accused persons were brought before the District Magistrate for the purpose of their confessions and statements being recorded. The Magistrate, L. Birley, took up the inquiry on 19 May.

The accused Sushil Chandra Sen was brought in custody on 20 May and his brothers Birendra Chandra Sen and Hem Chandra Sen were brought down to Calcutta and placed on their trial along with the others on 6 June 1908. The inquiry continued till 19 August 1908, when 30 accused were committed to the Court.

The Magistrate did not first commit the accused Barindra Kumar Ghose for trial with the other accused, but committed him on a separate charge for abetment of murder. Subsequently, in consequence of an order passed by the High Court, he committed him on the same charges as the rest.

The Confessional Statements

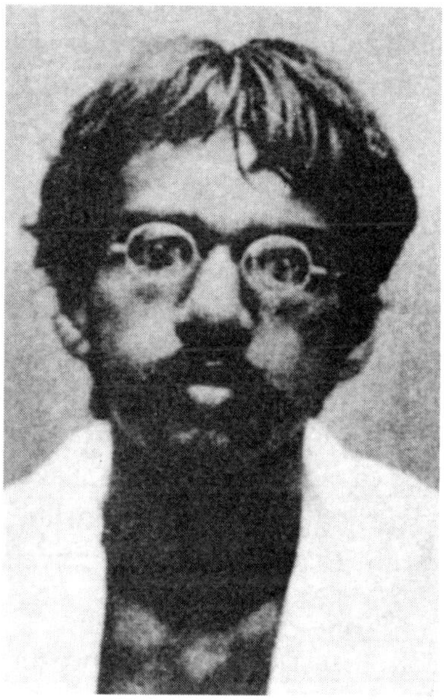

The signed statement of Barindra Kumar Ghose, aged about 28 years, made before L. Birley, Magistrate of the 1st class at Alipore, on the 4th day of May 1908, in the English language.

My name is Barindra Kumar Ghose. My father's name is Doctor Krishnadhan Ghose. I am by caste Kayastha, and by occupation formerly contributor to *Jugantar*. I was born at Croydon in England. I reside at 32 Muraripukur Road, Maniktola.

Do you wish to make a statement before me?
Yes.

Do you understand that your statement being made before a Magistrate will be admissible in evidence against you?
Yes.

Is your statement being made voluntarily or has any pressure been put upon you to make it?

No. It is quite voluntary.

Will you tell me what you have to say?
Whatever I had to say I have said in a written statement.

Have you any objection to making that statement to me here?
Shall I begin from the very beginning?

Yes.
In my statement I shall be a little vague about time because it is difficult to remember dates. I passed my entrance examination from the Deoghar School.

At what age did you come to India?
When I was one-year-old. After passing the entrance examination I went to Dacca where my brother Manomohan Ghose was Professor and I read up to the First Arts there. After that I gave up my studies and went to Baroda where my brother Aurobindo Ghose was a Professor in the Gaekwar's College. There I devoted myself to the study of History and Political Literature. After being there for a year I came back to Bengal with the idea of preaching the cause of independence as a political missionary. I moved about from district to district and started gymnasiums. There young men were brought together to learn physical exercises and to study politics.

I went on preaching the cause of independence for nearly two years. By that time I had been through almost all the Districts of Bengal, I got tired of it and went back to Baroda and studied for one year. I then returned to Bengal convinced that a purely political propaganda would not do for the country and that people must be trained spiritually to face dangers. I had an idea of starting a religious institution. By that time the *swadeshi* and boycott agitation had begun. I thought of taking men under my own instruction to teach them and so I began to collect this band which has been arrested. I started with my friend Abinash Bhattacharjee (now under arrest) and Bhupendra Nath Dutta (now in jail). I started the *Jugantar* paper. We managed it for nearly one-and-a-half years and then gave it over to the present managers.

After I gave it up, I again took to recruiting. I collected altogether 14 or 15 young men from about the beginning of 1907 until now. I educated the boys in religious books and politics. We are always thinking of revolution and wished to be ready for it, so we were collecting weapons in small quantities. Altogether I have collected 11 revolvers, four rifles and one gun. Among other young men who came to be admitted to our circle was Ullaskar Dutta; I don't remember exactly when but about the beginning of this year. He said that he wanted to come among us and be useful as he had learnt the preparation of explosives.

He had a small laboratory in his house without his father's knowledge and he experimented there. I never saw it ... he told me of it. With his help we began preparing explosives in small quantities in the Garden House at 32 Muraripukur Road. In the meantime another friend of ours, Hem Chandra Das of Kundrui in Midnapur District, after I think selling part of his property, went to Paris to learn mechanics and, if possible, explosives.

When did he go?
Approximately in the middle of 1907.

When did he return?
Three or four months ago, when he came back to join Ullaskar Dutta in preparing explosives and bombs.

Where did he do it?
At 38-4 Raja Nabakrishna Street, Calcutta, and at a house which he had rented in Bagh Bazar—15 Gopi Mohan Dutta Street. About five or six months ago, that is after press prosecution became numerous, we began to think of using explosives and wherever we went for money we were encouraged to use explosives. Thinking that to be the voice of the nation, we submitted and began serious preparations. The first attempt which we made was in French Chandernagore when the Lieutenant Governor was going to Ranchi. Ullaskar Dutt went to Chandernagore with a small dynamite mine and some fuse and detonators and tried to place it on the line just before the Special came. He was disturbed at the first place where he began by people coming out of their houses. He tried another place and could not place it properly and the Special came and he hurriedly dropped two or three cartridges and went away. There was a futile explosion.

What is your authority for this statement?
I sent him. I, Ullaskar and Upendranath Banerji used to do these things in consultation. I heard the account from Ullaskar. When the Lieutenant Governor was coming back from Cuttack two others started with a similar object—Prafulla Chandra Chaki of Bogra and Bibhuti Bhusan Sarkar (of Santipur, I believe). I went with them. We thought he would come back via Asansol. We went to Chandernagore.

What had you with you?
A mine and fuse. We waited but he did not come that way.

Did you lay the mine?
Yes.

Where?
Between Chandernagore and Mankundu Stations. As he did not come we picked it up and brought it away; we inquired at Chandernagore Station and we were told that the Lieutenant Governor was not coming that way. The third time we went on a similar errand to Kharagpur.

Who went?
The same three—I, Prafulla and Bibhuti. We left the train at Kharagpur at 10 a.m. In the afternoon we went by train to Narayangarh where we waited on the road which is parallel to the railway line. When it was dark we went to the railway line and waited till 9 p.m.

We waited at a spot about a mile from Narayangarh on the Kharagpur side. Here I shall give minute details because innocent people have been punished for this offence. We had with us a mine made of six pounds of dynamite charged in a thick iron vessel with a lid at the top. The lid had a hole in the centre. We had a fuse made of picric compound and powder was placed in a paper tube; we used a leaden pipe in case it should get choked by ballast. While we were placing the mine, the leaden pipe was found too long so we cut a piece off and threw it down there.

We had a dark lantern with candles. We had various things wrapped up in paper and we had copies of *Englishman* and of *Bande Mataram*; we also left them behind. They had stains of picric acid on them because the fuse was wrapped up in them. We had a cardboard shoebox that we left behind. We put cotton in the cardboard box and then a fuse and placed more cotton over it. We left the pieces of cotton behind.

We ate sweets there, near some bushes below the line, we left some *sal* leaves with the remnants of the food. We placed the mine there and, between 11 and 12 at night, I alone went back to Narayangarh and went by the last down passenger to Calcutta. I left behind the two boys and they placed the fuse on the line when the Special came. They said they were about one-and-a-half miles away when the explosion took place. We took no assistance from any *coolie* or anyone else.

After that there was a bomb outrage at Chandernagore. Hem Chandra Das prepared the bomb. Indu Bhusan Rai of Jessore and I and Narendra

Nath Gossain of Serampore went to Chandernagore together. We left the train at Mankundu Station at sunset. We went straight to Chandernagore Strand and waited till 10 p.m. We did not see the Mayor that night. We went and stayed the night under a tree near the station and the next morning Indra and Narendra went to Serampore to Narendra's place. Naren is the son of Nando Lal Gossami, Zamindar. I returned to Calcutta. We three went to Chandernagore again the same evening. I left the train there and Indra and Naren left at Mankundu. We met in the Strand and Indra undertook to throw the bomb.

He went to the window of the dining room where the Mayor was dining with his wife, which was on the ground floor in a bylane. He threw the bomb through the window gratings. We three went to Telinipara Ghat and crossed the river to Shamnagar and then to Calcutta. The bomb did not work; we came to the conclusion that the picric acid was bad. I was at a little distance when Indra threw it.

There is one more incident at Muzaffarpur and I shall explain it. Prafulla Chandra Chaki insisted on going with a bomb to Muzaffarpur to do away with Mr. Kingsford because he had tried the cases against the nationalist papers. The people in the country demanded his death. Hem Chandra and Ullaskar prepared the bomb at 15 Gopi Mohun Dutt's Lane. It was made of dynamite, put in a tin case with a wooden handle.

Upendranath and I consented to Prafulla going and Hem Chandra recommended Khudiram Bose of Midnapur. He was also allowed to go. I gave them two revolvers because they wanted to kill themselves if they were caught. Khudiram was an outsider. He did not know of the Garden House or of 15 Gopi Mohun Dutt's Lane.

He was staying with Hem Chandra Das. I took Prafulla from the Garden House, 32 Muraripukur Road to 15 Gopi Mohun Dutt's Lane and there he packed the bomb in a canvas bag and placed a revolver with it.

Where did you get the revolvers?
I do not wish to say. I took Prafulla to Hem's place and left him with Khudiram. I was told that they began the same night.

When were you arrested?
The day before yesterday, early in the morning.

Where?
At 32 Muraripukur Road.

Who else was there?
Ullaskar Dutt, Upendra Nath Banerji, Indra (Indu) Bhusan Rai, Bibhuti Bhusan Sarkar, Paresh Chandra Moulik, Nalini Kanta (Kumar) Gupta, Kunjo Lal Saha, Sachindra Nath Sen, Purna Chandra Sen, Hemendra Nath Ghose, Sisir Kumar Ghose, Bijoy Chandra Nag and others.

What were they doing there?
They are being instructed by me and Upendra Nath in religious and political books.

Do they live there?
Yes they were staying there with us.

How was this household supported?
I collected money from different people for supporting them. The object was to teach them and send out missionaries, and for this anarchical work.

What did the police find?
They found the weapons which I have mentioned and a quantity of dynamite and some bottles of nitric acid, sulphuric acid and picric acid. These things were buried in two iron tanks in the ground and in an earthen pot. The police found one and I pointed out the other two. There is one other thing which I can't tell you—the supporters' names.

Are any people out now on similar errands?
No. I also want to say that we are not responsible for shooting Mr. Allen nor for the Kustia shooting case.

Have you planned to destroy anyone else?
No. We have discussed destroying the Viceroy and the Commander-in-Chief but the plans took no practical form. We never believed that political murder will bring independence.

Then why do you do it?
We believe the people wanted it.

Stating the motive for disclosing the facts, Barindra Ghose said that his party was divided as to the propriety of disclosing these facts. He said: "Some thought they would deny everything and take the consequences but I persuaded them all to give written and oral statements to Inspector Ramsaday Mukerji because I believe that as this band was found out, it was best not to do any other work in the country, and because we ought to save the innocent." The Magistrate, Mr. L. Birley signed that the confession was voluntarily made; that it was taken in his presence and hearing and was read over to the person making it, and admitted by him to be correct and that it contained a full and true account of the statement made by him.

Barindra Ghose's statement was recorded in open court between 3 p.m. and 5 p.m. The accused was guarded by two constables of the Bengal Police and not by the Calcutta police constables who brought him. No other police officer was in Court. It is also pointed out that Barindra Ghose or Barin, as he was popularly known, had been in custody from the morning of Saturday, 2 May to the night of Sunday, 3 May and had written out a statement for the police too.

The statement of Bibhuti Bhusan Sarkar, aged about 20 years, made before L. Birley, Magistrate of the Ist class at Alipore, on the 4th day of May 1908, in the Bengali language.

My name is Bibhuti Bhusan Sarkar. My father's name is Sarada Prasad Sarkar. I am by caste Kayastha, and by occupation reading (studying), living in Muraripukur Garden.

My home is at Mouza Santipur, Sutragarh, Thana Santipur, District Nadia. I reside at Muraripukur Road, Maniktola.

I wish to make a statement. I understand that I am before a Magistrate and that what I say will be evidence against me. No one has compelled me to say anything. I have been living at Muraripukur Garden House since the time when the Lieutenant Governor was returning from Cuttack and there was a plot to put a bomb on the line.

What I know about that occurrence is that I dug a hole in the line by the side of the bridge. At that time Prafulla Chaki was with me. Barindra, Prafulla and I went to Chandernagore, but the L.G. did not come by the E.I.R. line. We waited from 4 p.m. till morning and then took the mine away because the Lieutenant Governor did not come. We had only made the hole and not put the mine in it.

After that when the L.G. had gone to Cuttack, Prafulla and I went by the Puri Passenger and left the train at Benapur at about 2.30 p.m.

From Benapur we walked in the direction of Narayangarh to look for a place to place a bomb. After going four miles we found a good place; we went to a place by the side of the road under a tree.

After 9 p.m. Prafulla and I went out to make a hole by the line and by 2.30 a.m. made it ready and walked to Kharagpur and returned to Calcutta by the Bombay Mail. On the day when the L.G. was expected, I and Barindra and Prafulla, with a mine and a lead pipe that Barin produced, went to Kharagpur in the Asansol Passenger.

We went on by the Puri Passenger to Narayangarh and then to the place where the hole was. The Lieutenant Governor did not come that day. We returned with the mine to Kharagpur; Prafulla and I waited at the waiting room and Barindra returned to Calcutta.

The next day Barindra came to us at Kharagpur with *Englishman* newspaper. From the paper we saw that the L.G. would come the next day. So, on the next day we went by the Puri Passenger, arriving at Narayangarh at 4 p.m.

At 8 p.m. we went to the hole and at 11 p.m. put the mine in the hole and Barin *Babu* returned at midnight to Calcutta by the Puri Passenger. Prafulla and I stayed till 2.35 a.m. At 2.30 a.m. we had placed the fuse on the line. We walked away towards Kharagpur. After going two miles we heard the explosion of the mine.

I did this because the Mohammedans opposed the Hindus at Jamalpur and Comilla and I learnt that it was done on behalf of the English.

The statement of Ullaskar Dutt, aged about 22 years, made before L. Birley, Magistrate of the lst class at Alipore, on the 4th of May 1908, in the English language.

My name is Ullaskar Dutt. My father's name is Durjadas Dutt. I am by caste Boidyo, and by occupation a cow keeper. My home is at Brahmanberia, District Tippera. I reside at Sibpur, Police Station, Sibpur, District Howrah.

Do you wish to make a statement to me?
Yes.

Do you understand that your statement being made before a Magistrate will be admissible as evidence against you?
Yes.

Is the statement made on account of any pressure being brought to bear upon you?
No. I should like to make the same statement as the written statement which I have given to the police.

Have you objection to making a statement orally to me?
No.

What is your story?

I had known Barindra Kumar Ghose for four or five years and nine or 10 months ago I joined his society.

What are the circumstances under which you joined?
It had been announced in *Jugantar* that a secret society would be started and I had a natural inclination to join. So I got introduced by Barindra.

What you used to do when you joined the society?
I used to prepare explosives.

When did you learn this?
Before I joined.

How?
I made a private laboratory of my own and tried experiments with small quantities.

Were you taught?
No.

What particular occurrences have you any information to give about?
I was present at a futile attempt at train wrecking at Chandernagore. I went alone and I took a mine made out of an iron cylinder with dynamite in it. I could not set it properly, because the train came up very quickly and I could not arrange it.

For whom was the mine intended?
For Sir Andrew Fraser's special train.

Who made that mine?
I myself. After that was the Kharagpur affair. I did not go to that. Barin, Bibhuti and Prafulla Chandra Chaki went. They took another mine.

Who made it?
I made it.

Where?
In a house in Goa Bagan in a lane of which I forget the name. We hired the house, perhaps Barin *Babu* hired it.

What was the mine like?
It was in a cast iron cylinder; it contained three pounds of dynamite. There was a fuse made of picric acid and chlorate of potash.

Did you make any explosives for use on any other particular occasion?
No.

Where were you arrested?
At 32 Muraripukur Road.

How long had you been there?
I used to go there for two or three days at a time and had been in the habit of doing so for about eight or 10 months.

What used to take place there?
We had a religious and moral training class for newcomers. I used to read the *Upanishad* there. I also used to prepare and experiment with explosives.

Did anyone else prepare and experiment with explosives?
Not there. Hem Chandra Das, who recently came from France, used to prepare explosives and bombs at his own place and at Gopi Mohun Dutt's Lane.

Have you anything else to say?
If you question me I can say.

Do you know anything about the Muzaffarpur outrage?
Yes. I know that Prafulla Chandra Chaki and Khudiram Bose went out for that purpose. I know because I was at Gopi Mohun Dutt's Lane, when they started about a week ago in the evening.

What did they take with them?
A bomb.

How did they take it?
In a canvas bag belonging to us and to nobody in particular.

Do you know who made the bomb?
I heard that Hem made it but I was not there when he made it.

Who are the leaders of the society?
There is no recognised leader, but Barin *Babu* acts as a leader.

Who are the members?
Barin, I, Hem Chandra Das, Upendranath Banerji, Indu Bhusan Rai, Prafulla Chandra Chaki, Bibhuti Bhusan Sarkar; these are the actual workers; there are others who were newcomers and used to be in the garden but have not been taken into confidence.

You say you made the mine for the Kharagpur affair. To whom did you give it?
To Barin *Babu*; he took it from the house at Goa Bagan.

I wish to add that the object of my confession is that innocent persons shall not suffer.

The statement of Indu Bhusan Rai, aged about 18 years, made before L. Birley, Magistrate of the lst class at Alipore, on the 4th of May 1908, in the English language.

My name is Indu Bhusan Rai. My father's name is Tarak Nath Rai. I am by caste Kayastha and by occupation *talukdar*. My home is at Mouza Sriphaltolla, Thana Khulna, District Khulna. I reside at 32 Muraripukur Road, Maniktola.

Do you wish to make a statement?
Yes. I have already made one.

Do you wish to make it to me, a Magistrate, knowing that it can be used as evidence against you?
Yes I understand.

Has any one put pressure to you to make a statement?
No.

What have you to say?
I have been living at 32 Muraripukur Road for a month-and-a half studying the *Gita* and preparing shells.

Under what circumstances did you first go there?
I met Barin *Babu* one-and-a-half months ago in College Square. I knew his name before. He told me there was a secret society and said he could allow me to join if I wished.

Did he say what its object was?
No. I knew already that its object was to make India free from the foreign yoke and to establish a better government.

Where were you educated?
I was taught at the Azeegara High School in Khulna District and in March 1907 I failed in the entrance examination. After that I was at home for two months and then I wandered about. I left home because my father wanted me to marry and I wished to live a life of a *brahmachari* (celibate). At Barin *Babu's* invitation I joined the society and went to live at 32 Muraripukur Road. A few days after I went there I began to prepare shells with Barin *Babu,* Bibhuti Sarkar and Prafulla Chaki.

Was anything done with these shells?
Yes. I have thrown a bomb in Chandernagore at the Mayor. I went with Barin *Babu* and a Serampore man whose name I do not know. I threw a bomb at 9 p.m. into the room where the Mayor was taking his food with his wife. The bomb did not burst. I ran away after I had thrown it. We three met together in the Strand Road and Barin *Babu* showed me the Mayor's house and then we three went near the Mayor's house and Barin and the Serampore man went into a lane.

Did you take part in any other occurrence?
No.

Have you anything else to say?
The main object of sacrificing my life is to set examples in the country.

Who taught you these ideas?
I got them from studying histories—Anandmath of Bankim Babu and Russian Revolutionary History.

The statement of Upendra Nath Banerjee, aged about 29 years, made before L. Birley, Magistrate of the Ist class at Alipore, on the 4th of May 1908, in the English language.

Do you wish to make a statement to me?
Yes.

Do you understand that if you make a statement to me, a Magistrate, the statement will be admissible as evidence against you?
Yes.

Has any pressure been used to get you to make a statement?
No.

What have you to say?
I passed the F.A. Examination from Dupleix College, Chandernagore, in 1898. I studied in Medical College, Calcutta, for two years and I gave up my studies through failure of health for one year and then joined the Duff College of Calcutta where I studied for about two years and then joined the Adwaita Ashram in Mayabati, Almora, for studying Hindu Philosophy and Yoga. After being there nearly two years I went home and was engaged as assistant headmaster in the Garbati High School, British Chandernagore. I stuck to the post for nearly one-and-a-half years and was then second master in the Bhadreswar English School for about a year. With a view to serve my country I gave up this post and joined the *Bande Mataram* staff as an assistant

editor. I had that post for nearly a year. At this time I was a regular contributor to *Jugantar*.

In order to carry out our work systematically I thought it necessary to found a sort of religious political society that would devote itself wholly to the cause of Indian regeneration but as I thought that the people of India would not be made to do any work except through religion, I wanted the help of some sadhus. I wandered about India looking for sadhus but couldn't find any. Failing sadhus, I fell back upon school boys and collected them to give them a religious, moral and political education.

Barindra Ghose had begun to collect youths and in September last I joined him. Since then I have been mainly engaged in teaching the boys about the state of our country and the need of independence and that the only way left for us is to fight for independence and to start secret societies in different parts of the country to propagate ideas and collect arms and rise in rebellion when the time shall be ripe. I knew that Barindra, Ullaskar and Hem were engaged in manufacturing bombs with a view to do away with the lives of those government officials who by repressive measures hampered our work—the Lieutenant Governor or Mr. Kingsford.

Barindra told me before he started that he was going to try to wreck the Lieutenant Governor's train at Kharagpur. When he came back, he said he had laid the mine. Bibhuti and Prafulla went with him. I know this because Barindra told me. He told me they had reported to him that it had been successful and they had heard a loud explosion.

Do you know anything about the Muzaffarpur outrage?
I heard from Birendra about a fortnight ago that Prafulla and Khudiram would be sent to Muzaffarpur to take Mr. Kingsford's life.

What did you say when you heard this?
I said nothing because I was not in charge of that department, but in charge of the education of the boys.

Was Prafulla under your instructions?
No. I used to teach the new recruits. I have made this statement because we agreed to tell the truth if arrested, so that the innocent might not suffer, and the successors may use greater caution.

Other Confessions

English translation of the statement of accused Narendra Nath Goswami made on the 5th of May 1908, before Mr. L. Birley.

Do you want to say anything before me?
Yes.

Do you understand that I am a Magistrate and whatever you will say before me may be taken as evidence against you?
Yes.

Has any one taught you anything by force?
No.

What do you want to say?
When the government at the time of the partition refused to listen to our petition, we tried to have *swaraj*. I made the acquaintance of Barin about two years ago. My heart was touched by reading *Jugantar*.

After the conviction of Bhupendra Nath Dutta, I tried to raise subscription to conduct the paper. I came to be acquainted with Hem Chandra Das, Upendra Nath Bannerjee and Ullaskar Dutt.

What did you do with them?
I didn't stay with them but held conversation with them on *swaraj*.

How was this society maintained?
I do not know. Barin was the head. He knows everything.

Did you do anything in particular?
I did. Barin came to me on the day next, previous to the bomb explosion in the Mayor's house, and asked me to see him in the Maniktola Garden the following day. Barin went away. I followed him the next day. From the garden I, Barin and another boy went to Hem Das's house at 2 or 3 p.m. I don't know the name of the boy. From there we started at 3 p.m. The boy was with us. He had a bag with him with three revolvers and a bomb.

We came to Howrah by tramcar and then went to Chandernagore. There we seated ourselves by the side of the Ganges. Three others joined us there from Chandernagore. I do not know them. Barin ordered one of them to look up what the Mayor was doing then.

He returned without any information. Nothing happened that day. We stayed that day in a house in Chandernagore. I had never been to the place before this and did not know the way well. When we went to the house there was a man there then. We three stayed there that night.

At about 4 in the night we came to Chandernagore Station, leaving our things there. I and the lad got into the same train and came down to Serampur. Barin went on to Calcutta. I and the lad went to my house.

At about 5.35 p.m. we got a carriage and went to Mankundu and then to Chandernagore. On reaching the *Ghat* we saw Barin with the three boys and the bag. Barin ordered one of the boys to see what the Mayor was doing. The boy returned and said that the Mayor had sat down to have his meal.

I then went towards the Mayor's house with the boy who had come with us from Calcutta and another boy. We (that is, I and the boy from Calcutta and another boy of Chandernagore) each had a revolver, in our hands. The boy who had come with us from Calcutta had also a bomb with him. Barin and the two others followed us at great distance.

When I was 50 yards off from the Mayor's house the boy ran up and threw the bomb into the house through the window. There was a sound then like that of a *pataka* (firecracker) and we three fled away to the side of the Ganges and came to Shamnagore in a ferry boat. We joined Barin on the Ganges side. At Shamnagore we took a carriage and came to Maniktola Garden. The next day in the morning I went to Serampur.

Why did you do this?
My blood became heated on reading *Jugantar*; that is, my mind underwent a change.

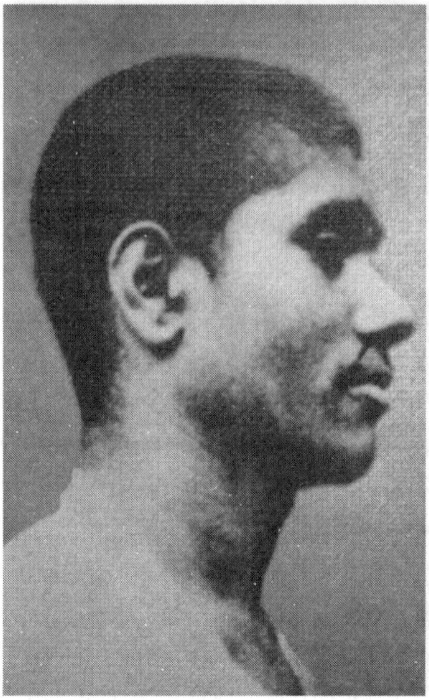

The statement of Sudhir Kumar Sarkar, aged about 18 years, made before L. Birley, Magistrate of the 1st class at Alipore, on the 11th of May 1908, in the English language.

Do you wish to make a statement to me?
Yes.

Do you understand that I am a Magistrate and that anything which you say can be used as evidence against you?
Yes.

Has any pressure been used to induce you to make a statement?
No.

Where were you at school?
I was a pupil at the Khulna Zilla School until nearly two years ago.

Why did you leave?
For two reasons, first because of the *swadeshi* agitation, and second because I failed in two subjects in a school examination.

What did you do then?
My father sent me to Sahebganj to my brother Narendra Kumar Sarkar, who was assistant jailor at Bhagalpur. My father wished me either to get employment in the University or continue my studies.

I had no mind to learn at the Calcutta University or to get an official employment. I therefore left my brother after about 15 days and went to Calcutta and became acquainted with Barindra Kumar Ghose.

When was that?
About a year-and-a-half ago.

How did you make his acquaintance?
I met him at the *Jugantar* office at 41 Champatola 1st Lane. I assisted at publishing the newspaper.

Who were managing it then?
Abinash Chandra Bhattacharjee was manager and also helping in the office were Upendra Nath Banerjee, Barindra Kumar Ghose, Dindayal and Sailendra Ghose. Dindayal was only living there; he was employed by the Tramways Company.

How long did you help in the office?
I lived there one month. I took no pay. Upendra gave me some books and I bought others on his recommendation, he instructed me to read them.

What books?
The works of Mazzini, Garibaldi, *Desherkatlia* by Sakharam Ganesh Deoskar, Bankim *Babu*'s works, Bhudeb *Babu*'s works (he was Director of Public Instruction), the *Upanishad*, the *Gita*. After being at the *Jugantar* office for one month, I went to Khulna and read these books there.

I spent most of my time at Khulna and occasionally came to Maniktola and used to stay for seven or eight days at a time in the Garden House of Barindra. I first got to know the Garden House while I was in the *Jugantar* office. Barindra took me there saying that there was a mission for religion and self-abnegation and political purposes.

Who used to live at the Garden House?
Upendranath Banerjee who used to teach me from the books named above. There also used to be Barindra, Sishir Kumar Ghose, Bejoy Kumar Nag. There were many others who used to come sometimes for a day at a time or a few hours. I cannot remember their names.

What were the political purposes of the mission?
To serve the motherland and to serve the people.

When did you last leave the Maniktola Garden House?
Nearly two months ago, since when I have been at Khulna, reading.

How do you support yourself?
I was supported by my father who is a government hospital assistant.

Have you anything else to say?
I intended to teach illiterate people religion.

How was the mission supported?
Barindra had a lot of money.

The statement of Hrishikesh Kanjilal, aged about 29 years, made before L. Birley, Magistrate of the Ist class at Alipore, on the 11th of May 1908, in the English language.

Do you wish to make a statement to me?
Yes.

Do you understand that I am a Magistrate and that your statement will be admissible as evidence against you?
Yes.

Has any pressure been put upon you to get you to make a statement?
No.

What is your statement?
I passed the entrance examination from the Baranagar Victoria School and F.A. from the General Assembly's Institution in Calcutta. I went in for B.A.

Examination from the Duff College and failed. While I was at Duff College I became acquainted with Upendra Nath Banerjee of Chandernagore who became my friend. When we were in the fourth year class we thought of renouncing this world and leading the lives of *sanyasi*s. Upen left college and went to Mayabati in Almora; after the examination I went to Benaras and stayed with my brother and studied Hindu Philosophy and Yoga.

I was about a year at Benaras and then I went to Mayabati and found my old friend Upendra Nath Banerjee there and I became acquainted with Ram Chandra Prabhu of Madras. I studied there Eastern and Western philosophy and so did my friends. When there was an earthquake at Kangra valley, Upen was sent to help the distressed. From there he went to Chandernagore, and when Lord Curzon trampled over the prayers and protests of the people and partitioned Bengal I decided to return to Bengal to serve the cause of my country instead of shutting myself up.

I was convinced that we must get freedom and that it was a sin not to stand against the tyranny and oppression of the government. I therefore came to Hardwar and preached *swadeshi* among the *sadhu*s and induced some of them to do the same. I was there a fortnight and then came to Benaras. There I received a letter from Upen and came to Gondalpara in Chandernagore. There Upen showed me a few copies of *Jugantar* and I studied them and I decided that we must secure the political independence of our country. I asked Upen to enquire in the *Jugantar* office whether there was really an organisation to free our country from the foreign yoke in Calcutta. That day I went to Chatra and I resolved to get a post in the education department so that I might preach to young boys the idea that it was by ceaseless hypocrisy and everlasting duplicity that the English had conquered our country. I got a post in Bhadreswar High English School. Four or five months later I heard from Upen that there was really a secret society at Calcutta under the leadership of Barindra Kumar Ghose, and he told me that he should join it soon. He was then also a teacher in the Bhadreswar English School. I then got a post at the Baidyabati School and Upen was appointed as assistant editor on the *Bande Mataram* staff.

Last summer, I went to the *Jugantar* office at 20 Champa Lane and I was introduced to Barindra by Upendra and thereafter I became friends with Barindra. He asked me to see him now and then. I returned home and afterwards I saw him at 24 Bagan Lane and I used to go to the Muraripukur Garden House. I went there four or five times.

What was going on there?
On one occasion when I was there, Barin told me that Upen was looking out for a suitable place to establish an ashram for imparting religious and political education to boys. On one occasion when I was at 24 Goa Bagan Lane I saw Barin, Ullaskar and another boy whose name I forget, they were ready to start for Chandernagore. I asked them what they would do and they told me that they were going to blow up the Lieutenant Governor's train.

While we were talking Narendra Nath Gossain of Serampore came there. We five went to Howrah Station and then in the evening towards Chandernagore. Barin asked Naren and me to help Ullaskar and the other boy by conducting them to Chatra. Naren and I alighted at Serampore and after sunset hired a carriage and went to Chandernagore. We left the carriage just opposite the Church and walked to Chandernagore Railway Station. There we waited two hours but did not find Ullaskar and the boy. But when we saw the Lieutenant Governor's Special passing safely, we heard only two reports—like those of cracking, between Mankundu and Chandernagore Railway Station. We waited there half-an-hour more, but finding that Ullaskar and the boy did not come we went home. After the Kharagpur incident I saw Barin and he told me that he, Prafulla Chaki and others went to Kharagpur and laid the mine.

On another occasion I was at the Muraripukur Road Garden House and there I saw Upen. We had a conversation about our organisation and Upen told me that bombs were being prepared. I asked who prepared them and where they were kept but Upen told me that I should know the whole thing when I became a permanent lodger in the Garden House and he asked me to join them shortly.

I had been at 23 Scott's Lane on one occasion and there I found Upen, Barin, Abinash Chandra Bhattacharji and a boy of Uttarpara who had come to take Aurobindo Ghose to Uttarpara for a lecture. Aurobindo was in the house upstairs. I say this because Barin told me and I also saw him come down and get into a carriage. That night Barin took me to 78 Russa Road, Bhawanipur and Upen accompanied us. I found four or five boys there whose names I did not enquire. Upen told Barin and me that the Mayor of Chandernagore had prevented a public meeting being held and that he should be taught a lesson. I stopped there for the night and I saw Ullaskar Dutt there. Next day I came home and two days after Narendra Nath Gossain of Serampore and a boy came to my house at Chatra and told me that they would go to kill the Mayor of

Chandernagore that night and asked me to provide lodging for the boy at night in my house.

The boy did not return to my house that night. After that I did not come to Calcutta because I had bad dysentery. I do not know about the Kingsford affair or the Allen shooting case, nor have I had any conversation with members of the society about those affairs.

Are you a member of the society?
I was not a registered member but I was to join them soon. I saw three revolvers when we went to Chandernagore. I was told by either Upen or Barin that Ullaskar was one of the bomb makers.

The statement of Birendra Nath Ghose, aged about 17-and-a-half years, made before L. Birley, Magistrate of the 1st class at Alipore, on the 15th of May 1908, in the English language.

Do you wish to make a statement to me?
Yes.

Do you understand that I am a Magistrate and that if you make a statement to me it can be used as evidence against you?
Yes.

Have the police ill-treated you in order to make a statement?
No.

What is your history?
My father is a small landowner. I have four brothers—Satyendra Nath, Dhirendra Nath, Sailendra Nath and Jitendra Nath.

Are any of the people who have been arrested related to you?
Hemendra Kumar and Sishir Kumar are the sons of my father's cousin. Aurobindo Ghose is the son-in-law of my cousin Bhupal Chandra Bose.

Where were you educated?
At Dibrugarh, which I left in October 1907. Then I went to Shillong to stay at the house of Bhupal Chandra Bose, Assistant Director of Land Records and Agriculture in Eastern Bengal. I went there with my nephew Sudhir Kumar Basu. I stayed till December and then went to Khulna to study at the National School. I stayed in Khulna with my cousin Hemanto Kumar Mazumdar who was a teacher in the school. He was transferred to Jessore National School about the end of December. After he left I stayed with Jatish Chandra Ghose, a pleader at Khulna who is a distant relation of mine. I did not join the school because I could not get a permanent place to stay after Hemanto left. I went to my home in January.

At the beginning of February I came to Calcutta with the mother of Jatish Chandra Ghose on the occasion of the Ardhodya Jog. In Calcutta, I stayed at 7 Hugal Kuria Lane, the house of Sirish Chandra Majumdar, a relative of Jatish and also at 46 Harrison Road with my brother Dhirendra Nath Ghose, who is a student at the Ripon College. Thence I returned home and came back to Calcutta after a few days.

Why did you return to Calcutta?
I wanted to study in the National College at Bowbazar Street, Calcutta, but I could not get a room in any mess.

I met Indu Bhusan Rai at Khulna in December. He used to visit Khulna, his home being near there. He used to associate with the students at Khulna. I met him again in February when I came to Calcutta. I was then staying at 46 Harrison Road. I met Indu Bhusan Rai on the road near 46 Harrison Road and he told me that there was an ashram in a garden at Manicktola, where the *Gita* and other Indian philosophy was taught by

Upendra Nath Banerjee. As I had a religious turn of mind I went with him to that garden.

When was that?
At the beginning of March.

What time of day did you go there?
About 2 p.m.

What did you find there?
I found some boys and young men there and talked with Upendra Nath Banerjee. He told me to read the *Gita* and other books, and asked me to visit the garden occasionally and to read there. I returned to 46 Harrison Road and went there again after about a week. I then stopped at the garden till the middle of March. I stayed day and night for five or six days. I was told that it was an ashram and that there was a regular class of *Gita* and other philosophical books. Upendra Nath Banerjee was the teacher.

Who else was living there?
Barindra Kumar Ghose, Bibhuti Bhushan Sircar, Ullaskar Dutt, Indu Bhusan Rai, Sachindra Kumar Sen, Bejoy Kumar Nag and one or two more whose names I do not know. Sachindra, Bejoy Kumar Nag and I regularly read *Gita* and the others studied privately.

I left the garden in about the middle of March and returned to 46 Harrison Road. I went home again. I came back again to 46 Harrison Road and went to Deoghar with Dhirendra, my brother; that was about 7 April. I stayed till May 9 or 10; I then went home on May 13 and was arrested on May 14 in the morning.

On how many occasions did you stay at the garden?
For about a week I went there daily and returned at night to 46 Harrison Road; for about a week I stayed there day and night.

Do you know what the object of the society there was?
I was given some hints that after one year's complete religious training I should have to serve my country.

How did you serve your country?
In any way in which Upendra Nath might describe; he told us that after a year's training we should be employed in work but did not say what kind of work, but I was given to understand that I was to sacrifice my life and other secular concerns and do nothing except serve the country.

Do you know what else was going on at the garden?
No.

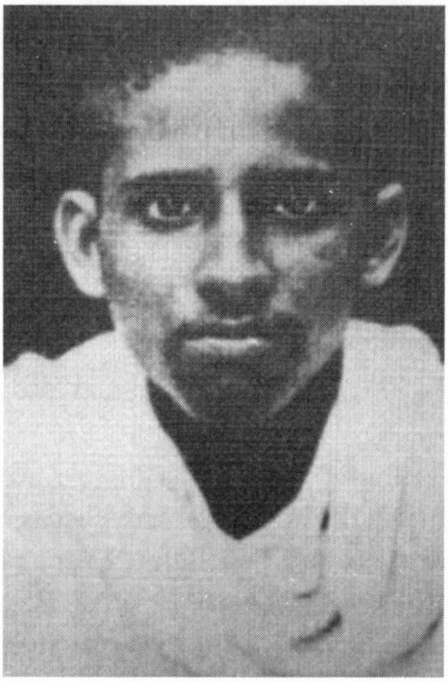

The statement of Kristo Jiban Sanyal, aged about 17 years, made before L. Birley, Magistrate of the Ist class at Alipore, on the 16th of May 1908.

Do you wish to make any statement to me?
Yes.

You know that whatever statement you will make before me will be evidence against you. I am a Magistrate.
Yes.

Has the police oppressed you in any way?
No.

What statement will you make?
I used to study in the Rajshahi Collegiate School up to September 1906. The Lieutenant Governor went to see the school in the month of July and about 135 students did not go to school because we did not want to make *salaam* to Fuller Saheb. For this reason five students were expelled, namely, I, Narendra Buxi, Girija Kanto, Mukutmani and Anantalal Roy.

What happened after that?
I went to study in the Rungpur National School. I was a student there from the month of *Aughran* (November and December) till the month of *Joisto* (May and June). From there I went home. I read about the Giridih National School in the *Navasakti*. On hearing this I wrote a letter to Naren Buxi as to whether he should study there. He consented. I went to study at Giridih. Naren went a week later. We studied there from the month of *Sraban* (July and August) till the month of *Aswin* (October and November). After that we went home during the *pooja* vacation. After the vacation we again went to study in Giridih. We studied there up to the month of *Baisakh* (April and May). After appearing at the examination I wrote to Paresh Chandra Moulik that I was going to Calcutta. I made the acquaintance of Paresh at Rungpur. After writing the letter I came to Calcutta with Naren Buxi and on arrival there I stayed at a mess in 44/3 Harrison Road for about two or three hours. Paresh Chandra Moulik came there. I and Naren went with him to the Maniktola Garden House. I stayed there for 15 days and used to remain there day and night.

Who were there?
Upendra Nath Banerjee, Barindra Nath Ghose, Narendra Nath Buxi, Bibhuti, Indro, Sachin, Paresh, Ullas Dutt and Prafulla Chaki.

What was taking place there?
Barin Ghose used to read the *Gita* to me and Upen Banerjee used to read the *Upanishads* to me. Barin also used to read about the Russo-Japanese War. Ullas Dutt delivered lectures regarding explosives on two days.

How many of you were present when Ullaskar delivered lectures about explosives?
All those who were then staying at the Garden House were present.

What was the object of those persons?
To learn the *Gita* and the *Upanishad* and work for the strength and good of the country.

Did you see anything in the garden?
I saw a long gun inside the room.

When you were staying there, did anyone leave the place to do any work?
Prafulla Chaki went out with Barin. Four days after they left I went home. We went with Nirmal one day to Bhowanipore. He went to engage a house there for our men. A house was available, but was not engaged.

During the course of inquiry the government tendered pardon under Section 337 Criminal Procedure Code to Narendra Nath Gossain to become an approver in the case. On 23 June 1908 Narendra Nath Gossain was discharged under Section 209, Criminal Procedure Code, but detained in custody for being examined as a witness for the Crown.

About 222 witnesses were examined by the Crown from 19 May to 15 August 1908. When the inquiry in the case was coming to a close, the District Magistrate passed the following orders on 15 August 1908:

> Examined witness No. 222. No more witnesses present. At this stage Counsel for the Prosecution informed that he has certain other evidence which he desires to produce at the trial, it was referred to be of two types: (i) Translation of correspondence, books and reports and explanations of manuscript plans already admitted in evidence, etc. (ii) New evidence including evidence of searches of houses of certain of the accused who were sent up after this trial began but are not before me.
>
> It was proposed that if satisfied with the evidence I should cómmit the accused without first taking this evidence and Counsel for Defence being asked whether the Defence objects does not express any opinion. The evidence as a matter of fact has been already admitted and I should not record further evidence before commitment and the High Court would decide whether this further evidence is to be admitted.[sic]
>
> The accused were asked whether they wish to make any further statements, evidence having been taken after their examination. None of them wish to make further statements.

Of the original 33 persons named in the First Information Report initially filed by Inspector Puran Chandra Biswas of CID, Bengal, the High Court had already passed the death sentence on Khudiram Bose on 13 July 1908. He was hanged for his role in the Muzaffarpur bombing on 11 August 1908. With Narendra Nath Gossain already having turned approver, it left 31 people, including Barindra Kumar Ghose.

On 19 August 1908, District Magistrate, L. Birley, committed 30 accused persons under Sections 121, 121A and 123 IPC for trial by the Court of Sessions. The same day, Birley also drew up the charges:

> First. That you on or about the 12 months preceding 15 May 1908 at various places in Bengal, including 32 Muraripukur Road, Maniktola, which is in my jurisdiction, did wage war against the King, attempted to wage war against the King and abetted the

waging of war against the King and thereby committed an offence punishable under Section 121 of the Indian Penal Code and within the cognisance of the Court of Sessions.

Secondly. That you on or about the 12 months preceding 15 May 1908 at various places in Bengal, including 32 Muraripukur Road, Maniktola, did conspire to wage war against the King and to deprive the King of the sovereignty of British India and did conspire to overawe by criminal force the Government of India and the local Government of Bengal and thereby committed an offence punishable under Section 121A of the IPC and within the cognisance of the Court of Sessions.

Thirdly. That you on or about the 12 months preceding 15 May 1908 at various places in Bengal, including 32 Muraripukur Road, Maniktola, did by illegal omissions conceal the existence of a design to wage war against the King, intending and knowing that by such concealment you would facilitate the waging of such war and thereby committed an offence punishable under Section 123 of the Indian Penal Code and within the cognisance of the Court of Sessions. And I hereby direct that you be tried by the said Court on the said charges.

Signed: L. Birley, District Magistrate (24 Parganas)

Informing Barindra Kumar Ghose that he would be tried for abetment of murder, Birley explained to him that if Barindra claimed his rights as a European British subject he would be tried by the High Court and, if not, then by the Sessions Court. Barindra did not claim the right. In Barindra's case, District Magistrate Birley was also of the opinion that since the accused had committed specific offences, the accused should first be tried for committing such offences in preference to trying him in connection with the general conspiracy. In his view, it was proper that the accused Barindra should first be tried for the individual offence and should therefore be declined to trial under Sections 121, 121A and 123 IPC.

On 26 August 1908, an application was, however, made before the District Magistrate on behalf of the Prosecution, asking to commit Barindra Kumar Ghose under Sections 121, 121A and 123 IPC, along with the 30 other accused already committed. On 2 September 1908, the High Court passed the order that the Magistrate either discharge Barindra or commit him for trial under Sections 121, 121A and 123 IPC. The Magistrate informed Barindra Kumar Ghose that he would be charged under Sections 121, 121A and 123 IPC. And, as Barindra had declined to claim his right as a European British subject, he was committed for trial by the Court of Sessions.

Revenge on 'The Traitor'

All the arrested persons—including Narendra Nath Gossain who had turned government approver—had meanwhile been lodged in the Alipore Jail in Calcutta. Pardoned by the government, in the eyes of the revolutionaries Narendra Nath Gossain was an unpardonable traitor who had betrayed the secret society's trust.

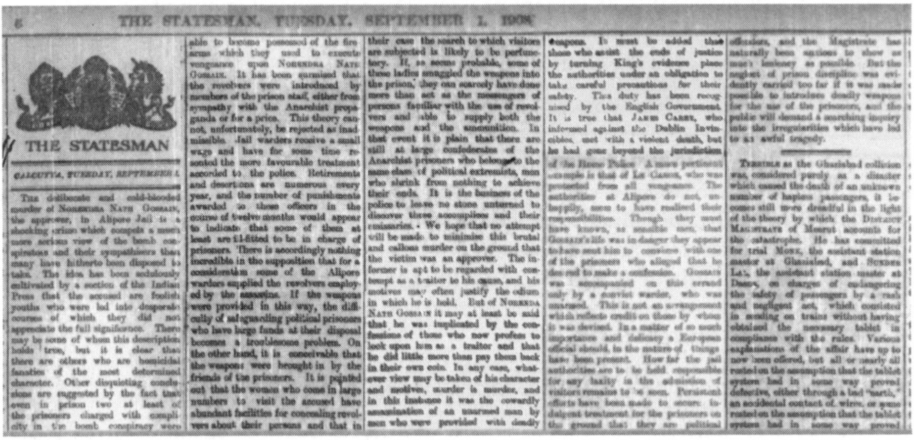

6 THE STATESMAN, TUESDAY, SEPTEMBER 1, 1908

THE STATESMAN

CALCUTTA, TUESDAY, SEPTEMBER 1

The deliberate and cold-blooded murder of Norendra Nath Gossain, the approver, in Alipore Jail is a shocking crime which compels a much more serious view of the bomb conspirators and their sympathisers than many have hitherto been disposed to take. The idea has been sedulously cultivated by a section of the Indian Press that the accused are foolish youths who were led into desperate courses of which they did not appreciate the full significance. There may be some of whom this description holds true, but it is clear that there are others who are homicidal fanatics of the most determined character. Other disquieting conclusions are suggested by the fact that even in prison two at least of the prisoners charged with complicity in the bomb conspiracy were able to become possessed of the fire-arms which they used to execute vengeance upon Norendra Nath Gossain. It has been surmised that the revolvers were introduced by members of the prison staff, either from sympathy with the Anarchist propaganda or for a price. This theory cannot, unfortunately, be rejected as inadmissible. Jail warders receive a small wage and have for some time resented the more favourable treatment accorded to the police. Retirements and desertions are numerous every year, and the number of punishments awarded to these officers in the course of twelve months would appear to indicate that some of them at least are ill-fitted to be in charge of prisoners. There is accordingly nothing incredible in the supposition that for a consideration some of the Alipore warders supplied the revolvers employed by the assassins. If the weapons were provided in this way, the difficulty of safeguarding political prisoners who have large funds at their disposal becomes a troublesome problem. On the other hand, it is conceivable that the weapons were brought in by the friends of the prisoners. It is pointed out that the women who come in large numbers to visit the accused have abundant facilities for concealing revolvers about their persons and that in their case the search to which visitors are subjected is likely to be perfunctory. If, as seems probable, some of these ladies smuggled the weapons into the prison, they can scarcely have done more than act as the messengers of persons familiar with the use of revolvers and able to supply both the weapons and the ammunition. In that event it is plain that there are still at large confederates of the Anarchist prisoners who belong to the same class of political extremists, men who shrink from nothing to achieve their ends. It is the business of the police to leave no stone unturned to discover these accomplices and their emissaries. We hope that no attempt will be made to minimise this brutal and callous murder on the ground that the victim was an approver. The informer is apt to be regarded with contempt as a traitor to his cause, and his motives may often justify the odium in which he is held. But of Norendra Nath Gossain it may at least be said that he was implicated by the confessions of those who now profess to look upon him as a traitor and that he did little more than pay them back in their own coin. In any case, whatever view may be taken of his character and motives, murder is murder, and in this instance it was the cowardly assassination of an unarmed man by men who were provided with deadly weapons. It must be added that those who assist the ends of justice by turning King's evidence place the authorities under an obligation to take careful precautions for their safety. This duty has been recognised by the English Government. It is true that James Carey, who informed against the Dublin Invincibles, met with a violent death, but he had gone beyond the jurisdiction of the Home Police. A more pertinent example is that of Le Caron, who was protected from all vengeance. The authorities at Alipore do not, unhappily, seem to have realised their responsibilities. Though they must have known, as sensible men, that Gossain's life was in danger they appear to have sent him to converse with one of the prisoners who alleged that he desired to make a confession. Gossain was accompanied on this errand only by a convict warder, who was unarmed. This is not an arrangement which reflects credit on those by whom it was devised. In a matter of so much importance and delicacy a European official should, in the nature of things have been present. How far the jail authorities are to be held responsible for any laxity in the admission of visitors remains to be seen. Persistent efforts have been made to secure indulgent treatment for the prisoners on the ground that they are political offenders, and the Magistrate has naturally been anxious to show as much leniency as possible. But the neglect of prison discipline was evidently carried too far if it was made possible to introduce deadly weapons for the use of the prisoners, and the public will demand a searching inquiry into the irregularities which have led to an awful tragedy.

Terrible as the Ghaziabad collision was, considered purely as a disaster which caused the death of an unknown number of hapless passengers, it becomes still more dreadful in the light of the theory by which the District Magistrate of Meerut accounts for the catastrophe. He has committed for trial Mohr, the assistant station master at Ghaziabad, and Sunder Lal, the assistant station master at Dasna, on charges of endangering the safety of passengers by a rash and negligent act, which consisted in sending on trains without having obtained the necessary tablet in compliance with the rules. Various explanations of the affair have up to now been offered, but all or nearly all rested on the assumption that the tablet system had in some way proved defective, either through a bad "earth," an accidental contact of wires, or some rested on the assumption that the tablet system had in some way proved

The Statesman, Calcutta, Tuesday, September 1, 1908, Page 5

The revolutionaries were, therefore, always on the lookout for an opportunity to kill him. And this killing they decided to carry out without much delay in Alipore Jail itself, right under the nose of the British. The task was assigned to Kanai Lal Dutt and Satyendra Nath Bose. Somehow, they managed to smuggle two revolvers into the jail ... And on 31 August 1908, in the Alipore Central Jail Hospital, they succeeded in attacking and killing Narendra Nath Gossain. In a statement given to the press representative, the Jail Superintendent had said:

> At about 7 a.m. on Monday morning, Satyendra Nath Bose of Midnapore and Kanai Lal Dutt of Chandernagore sent word to the authorities from the jail hospital, where they were confined as sick prisoners, that they wished to make a confession. The approver Narendra Nath, with a European convict warder named Higgins, went to the two men to sound them. As soon as they got to the door of the hospital, the two men rushed out—each armed with a revolver—and opened fire on the approver, who ran away in the direction of the mill. Higgins and later another European prisoner named Linton tried to prevent the two armed men from

following when the accused immediately fired at them, with the result that both of them were injured—Higgins in the right wrist and Linton in the head.

Then the accused again rushed up and, getting quite close to the approver, fired point blank at his back. The bullet hit Narendra. He fell into a drain by the side of the bathroom. He was found to be senseless and apparently dying. The alarm was at once given and the District Superintendent of Police, Alipore, went immediately with a force of Alipore Reserve Police and the two men were arrested and charged with murder and attempted murder. Narendra Nath Gossain was carried to the hospital where the

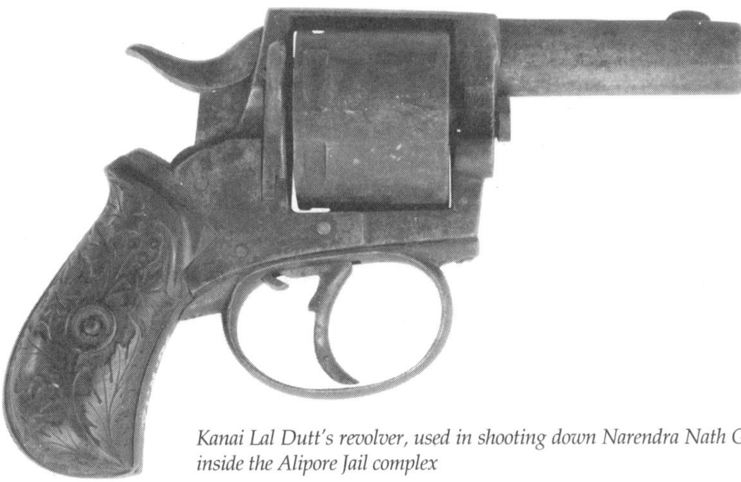

Kanai Lal Dutt's revolver, used in shooting down Narendra Nath Gossain inside the Alipore Jail complex

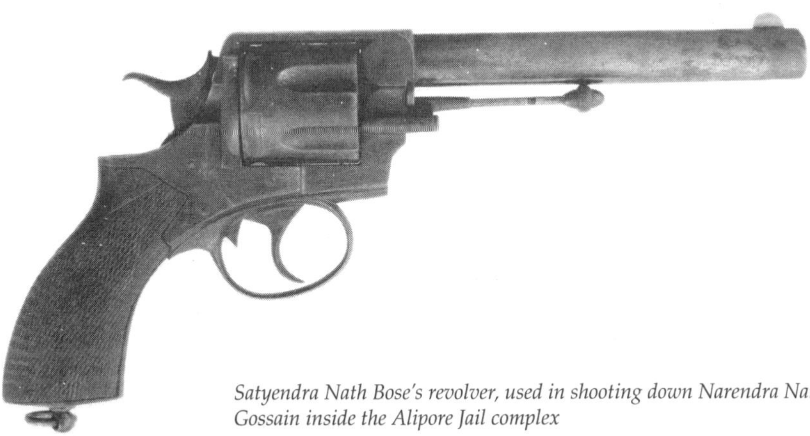

Satyendra Nath Bose's revolver, used in shooting down Narendra Nath Gossain inside the Alipore Jail complex

> assistant tried some remedies, but in vain. He was declared dead. How the prisoners managed to get weapons inside the jail premises remains a mystery. But the day before was visiting day and the prisoners had received a large number of visitors.

The postmortem examination on the body conducted by Dr. Daly showed five distinct wounds. Only one bullet was extracted. The examination showed that the bullet that caused Gossain's death had entered his back just beneath the left shoulder blade, pierced the vertebrae, severing the spinal cord, passed through the right lung and finally exited beneath the skin on the right chest.

The weapons used in committing the murder were of two types. One of the revolvers that was used by Kanai Lal Dutt was a 3.80 bore Charles Osborne while the other was a Royal Irish Constabulary 4.50 bore Webley. While the former was small, the latter was large and cumbrous.

The murder of Narendra Nath Gossain within the Alipore Jail precincts created a furore in British as well as nationalist circles, although of the opposite kinds. The government instituted an inquiry to discover the laxity on the part of administration as to how such an incident could occur within the jail premises. Submitted in November 1908, the report drew attention to the worrying facts that at least two revolvers with ammunition were in the hands of prisoners in the jail; that prisoners in sufficiently good health to commit a desperate murder were admitted in the jail hospital and that an approver from among the original group was able to associate with those against whom he had given—and was to give—evidence. Justifying the strong public comments on this laxity of discipline within the jail, it called for a searching enquiry into the circumstances that made the murder possible.

It was admitted that the murder of Narendra Nath Gossain was made possible by gross dereliction of duty on the part of the principal medical subordinate of the Alipore Jail, added to serious carelessness and neglect on the part of the medical officer and that the Superintendent and the jailor contented themselves with carrying on the work of their offices in a mechanical manner according to recognised routine and failed to rise to an emergency or to show that degree of sense of responsibility and devotion to duty which the government expects from its officers.

The government mulled over certain concerns that were raised regarding whether the procedures followed in the Bengal jails were adequate enough to meet the onslaught of gangs of desperate criminals, belonging to the educated classes and supported by numerous and influential sympathisers outside the jail walls, such as the recent politico-criminal movement had been brought to being. The Inspector-General of Prisons was directed to consider the changes demanded by the new situation and to submit his proposals to the government.

Kanai Lal Dutta, one of the revolutionaries who shot dead Narendra Nath Gossain

Mr. Marr, the District Magistrate of 24 Parganas, completed the enquiry into the circumstances leading up to incident at the Alipore Jail. In all, 19 witnesses were examined. Principal among them were two European convict-cum-warders, Higgins and Linton, and Dr. Daly, the doctor who had conducted the postmortem examination on the body of Narendra Nath Gossain. Kanai Lal Dutt and Satyendra Nath Bose were tried for the murder of Narendra Nath Gossain and subsequently held guilty and hanged. Meanwhile, some other persons connected with the Alipore Bomb Case were also arrested and formed a second batch. A preliminary enquiry was made by the District Magistrate L. Birley who charged them under Sections 121, 121A and 123 IPC and on 14 September 1908 committed them to take their trial before the Court of Sessions, along with the other accused.

The trial of both the batches commenced before Charles Porten Beachcroft, ICS, Additional Sessions Judge, Alipore, on 19 October 1908. It came to be known as the Alipore Bomb Conspiracy Trial.

Charging all the accused in the Alipore Bomb Conspiracy Case, the judge read the charges before the accused. The crux of the charges were as follows:

1. Waged war against His Majesty the King-Emperor of India and thereby committed an offence punishable under Section 121 of the Indian Penal Code.
2. Attempted to wage war against His Majesty the King-Emperor of

Charles Porten Beachcroft, ICS, Additional Sessions Judge, Alipore

India, and thereby committed an offence punishable under Section 121 of the Indian Penal Code.

3. Abetted one another, and other persons, in waging war against His Majesty the King-Emperor of India, and thereby committed an offence punishable under Section 121 of the Indian Penal Code.

4. Conspired among yourselves, and with other persons, to commit all or any of the offences under Section 121 of the Indian Penal Code, as set forth in the above three counts, and thereby committed an offence punishable under Section 121A of the Indian Penal Code.

5. Conspired among yourselves, and with other persons, to deprive His Majesty the King-Emperor of India of the Sovereignty of British India or of a part thereof, and thereby committed an offence punishable under Section 121A of the Indian Penal Code.

6. Conspired among yourselves and with other persons to overawe by criminal force the Government of India or the Local Government of Bengal, and thereby committed an offence punishable under Section 121A of the Indian Penal Code.

7. Collected men, arms or ammunitions or otherwise prepared to wage war with the intention of either waging or being prepared to wage war against His Majesty the King-Emperor of India and thereby committed an offence punishable under Section 122 of the Indian Penal Code.

8. Concealed by illegal omissions the existence of a design to wage war against His Majesty the King-Emperor of India, intending by such concealment to facilitate, or knowing it to be likely that such concealment would facilitate, the waging of such war, and thereby committed an offence punishable under Section 123 of the Indian Penal Code.

The defence and the prosecution were represented by eminent barristers—Mr. Chittaranjan Das (who was instrumental for the acquittal of Aurobindo Ghose and became a nationalist leader popularly known as 'Desh Bandhu') and Mr. Eardley Norton (known as the Lion of Madras Corporation).

On behalf of the defence, as many as 11 substantial legal objections regarding jurisdiction, charges, evidence and witnesses, the method and manner of searches were taken.

All these objections were overruled and Mr. Eardley Norton opened the case for the Crown, which took him six days.

The Evidence

Two-hundred-and-six witnesses were examined and cross-examined at length on behalf of the Crown by Eardley Norton and a large number of exhibits were also produced in the court. Due to the high volume of the material it is not possible to give reference to all in this book. Here, I am concentrating on the material that was said to be significant in acquitting Aurobindo Ghose, who was considered to be a principal accused in the case.

Exhibit 283: 'The Morality of Boycott'

(Excerpts from the unpublished article written for Bande Mataram*)*

> If the British exploitation were to cease tomorrow, the hatred against the British race would disappear in a moment. A partial *adhyaropa* makes the ignorant for the moment see in the exploiters and not in the exploitation the receptacle of the hostile feeling. But like all *maya*, it is an unreal feeling and sentiment and is not shared by those who think. Not hatred against foreigners, but antipathy to the evils of foreign exploitation is the true root of boycott.
>
> If hatred is demoralising, it is also stimulating. The web of life has been made a mingled strain of good and evil and God works His ends through the evil as well as through the good. Let us discharge our minds of hate, but let us not deprecate a great and necessary movement because, in the inevitable course of human nature, it has engendered feelings of hostility and hatred. If hatred came, it was necessary that it should come as a stimulus, as a means of awakening.
>
> When *tamas*, inertia, torpor have benumbed a nation, the strongest forms of *rajas* are necessary to break the spell; there is no form of *rajas* so strong as hatred. Through *rajas* we rise to *sattva* and for the Indian temperament the transition does not take long. Already the element of hatred is giving place to the clear conception of love for the Mother as the spring of our political actions. Another question is the use of violence in the furtherance of boycott. This is, in our view, purely a matter of policy and expediency. An act of violence brings us into conflict and may be inexpedient for a race circumstanced like ours. But the moral question does not arise.
>
> The argument that to use violence is to interfere with personal liberty involves a singular misunderstanding of the very nature

The following accused were tried on the eight charges:

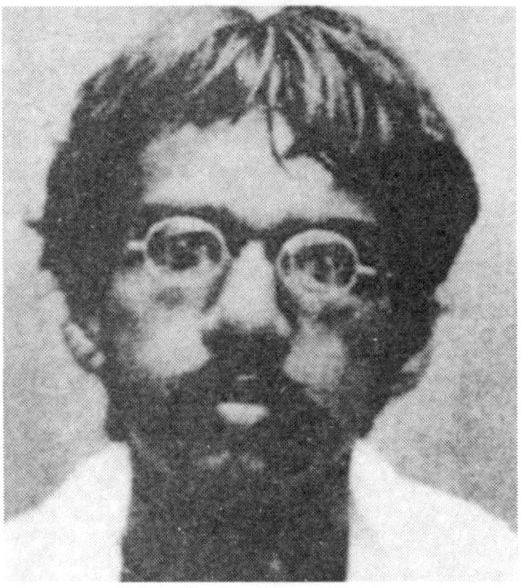

Barindra Kumar Ghose

Indu Bhusan Rai

Ullaskar Dutt

Upendra Nath Banerjee

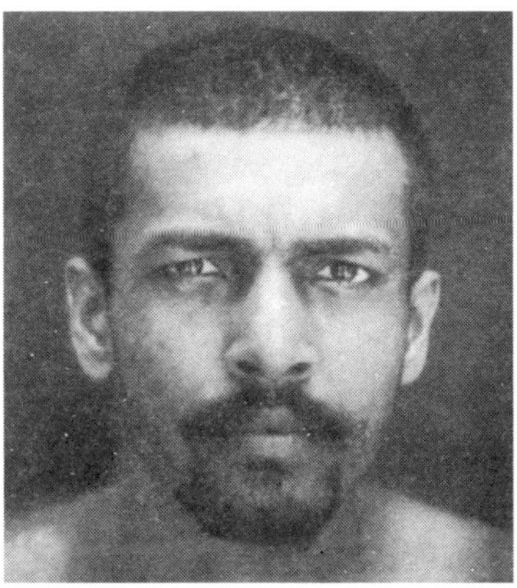

Sishir Kumar Ghose

Nalini Kumar Gupta

The accused (continued):

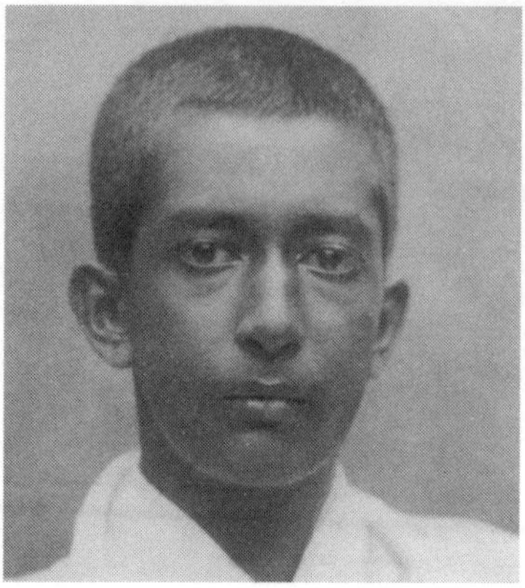

Sachindra Kumar Sen

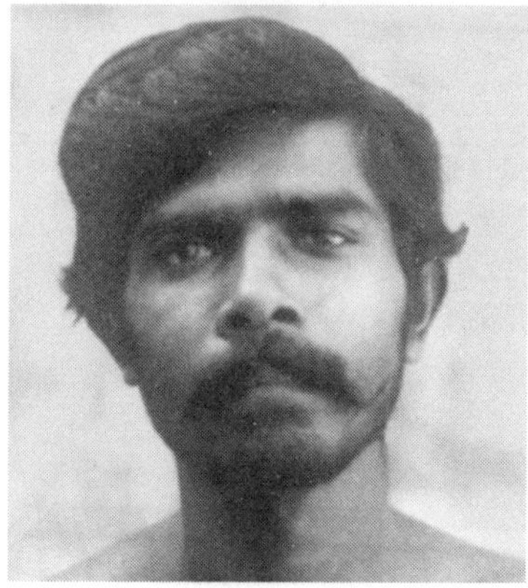

Paresh Chandra Moulik

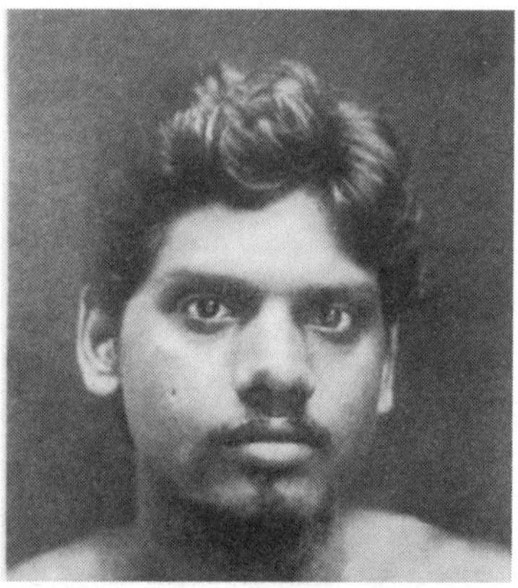

Kunja Lall Shaha

Bijoy Kumar Nag

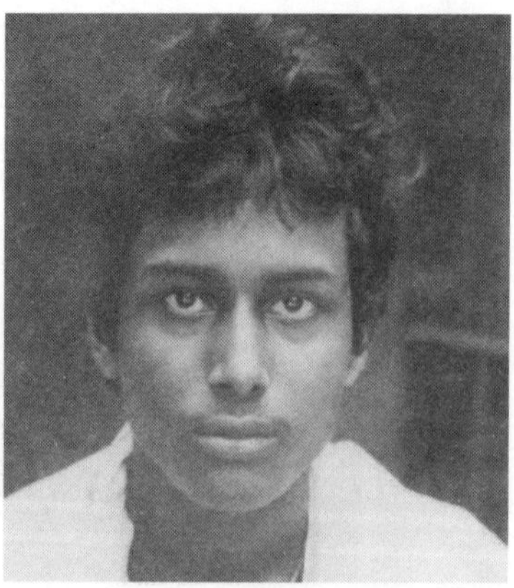

Narendra Nath Bakshi

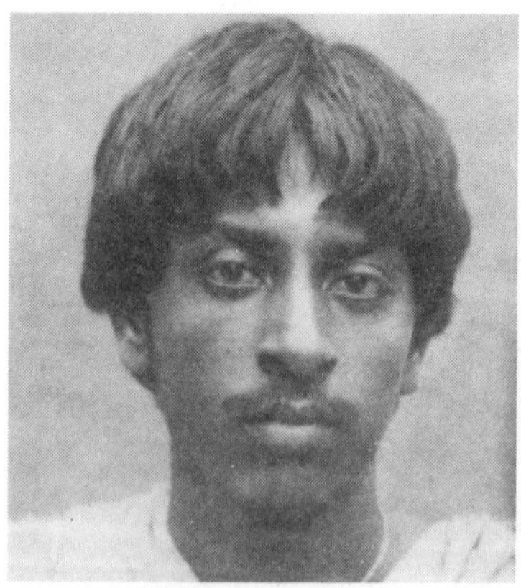

Purna Chandra Sen

The accused (continued):

Hemendra Nath Ghose

Bibhuti Bhushan Sarkar

Nirapodo Rai

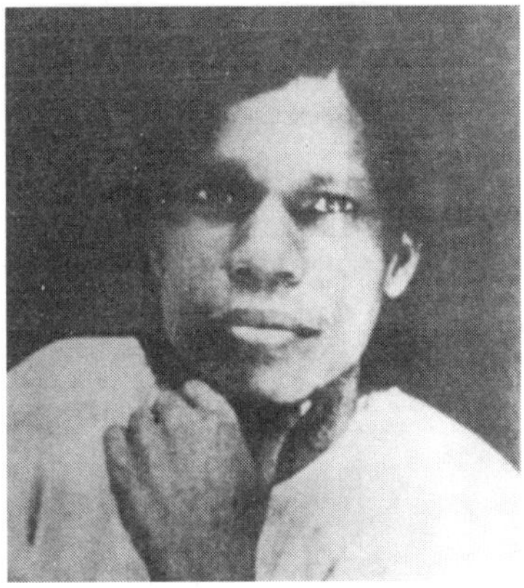

Hem Chandra Das

Aurobindo Ghose

Abinash Chandra Bhattacharji

The accused (continued):

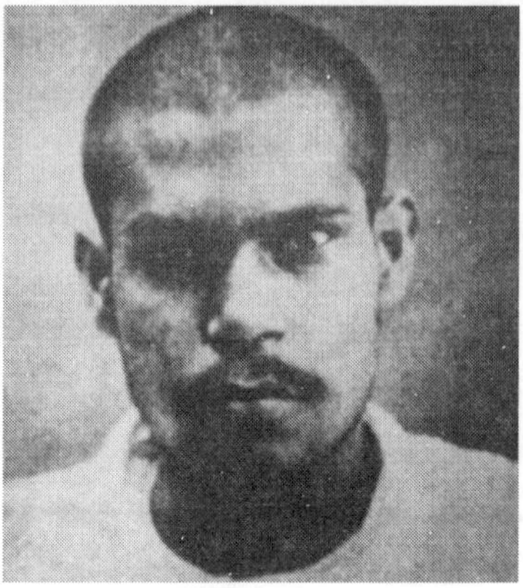

Sailendra Nath Bose

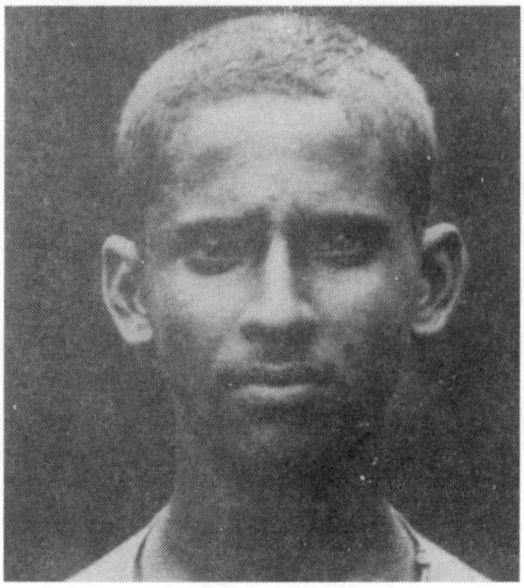

Krishna (Kristo) Jiban Sanyal

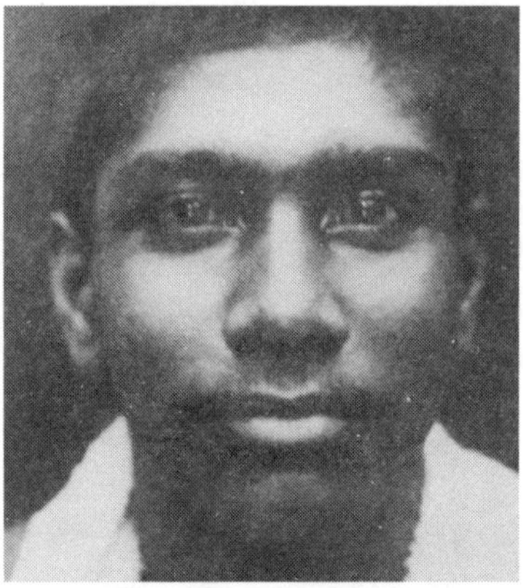

Sudhir Kumar Sarkar

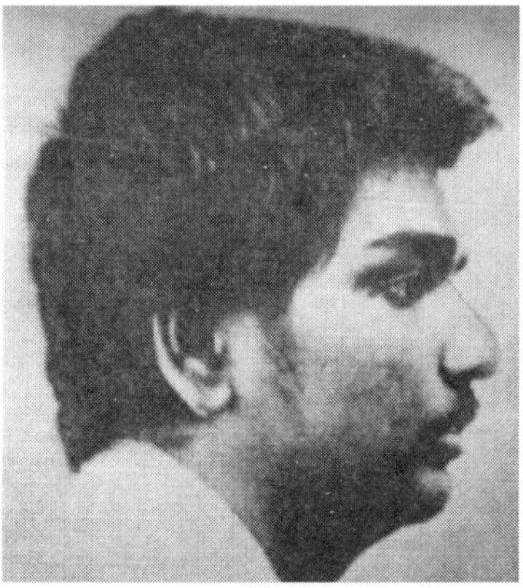

Birendra Nath Ghose

Hrishikesh Kanjilal

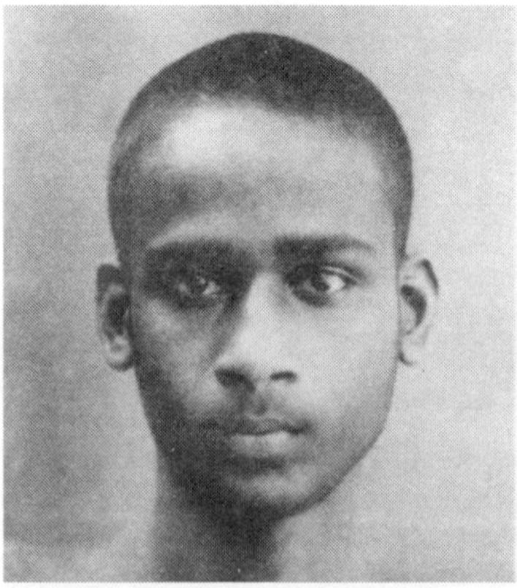

Birendra Chandra Sen

The accused (continued):

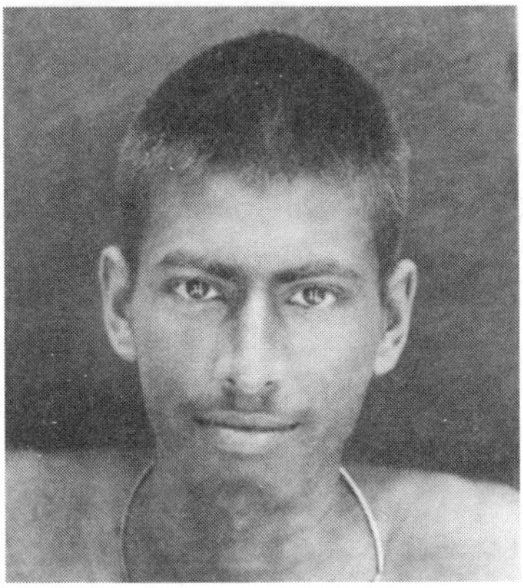

Dharani Nath Gupta

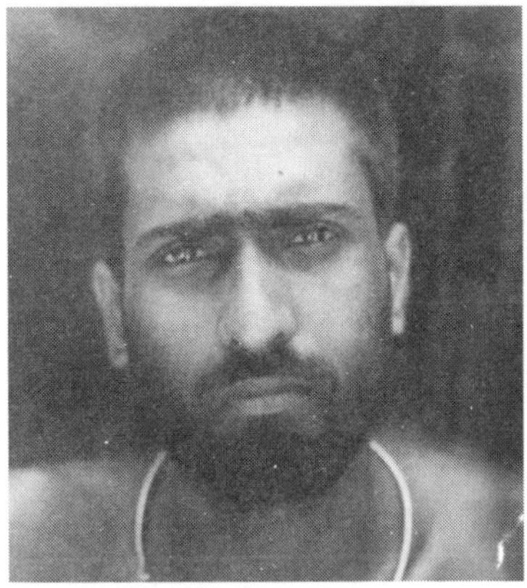

Nogendra Nath Gupta

Asoke Chandra Nandy

Sushil Kumar Sen

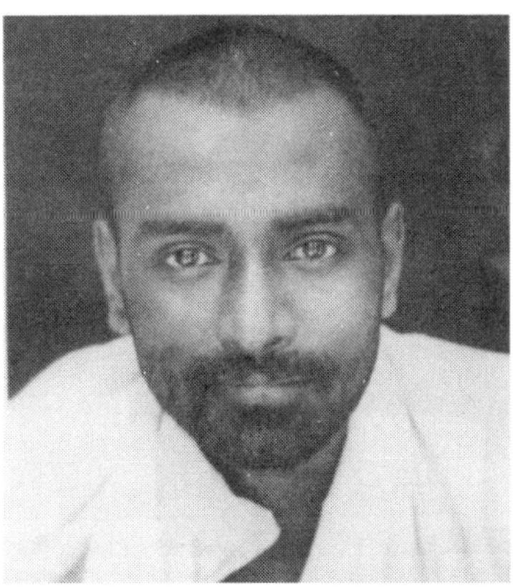

Provash Chandra Deb alias Manik Lal Deb

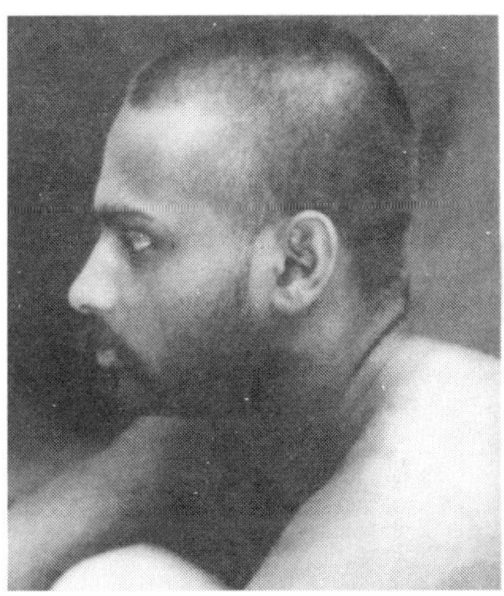

Hem Chandra Sen

The accused (continued):

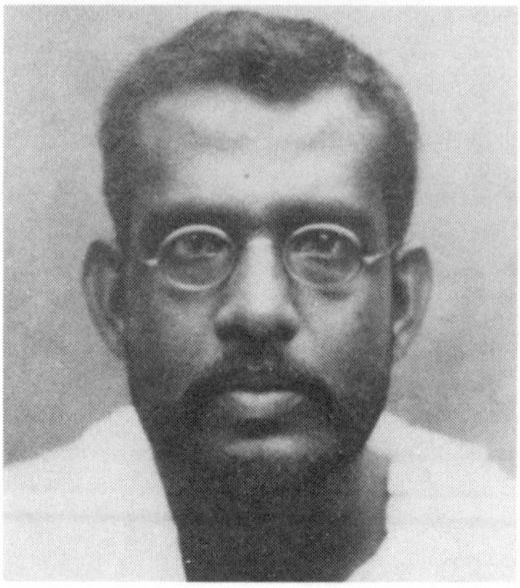

Debabrata Bose

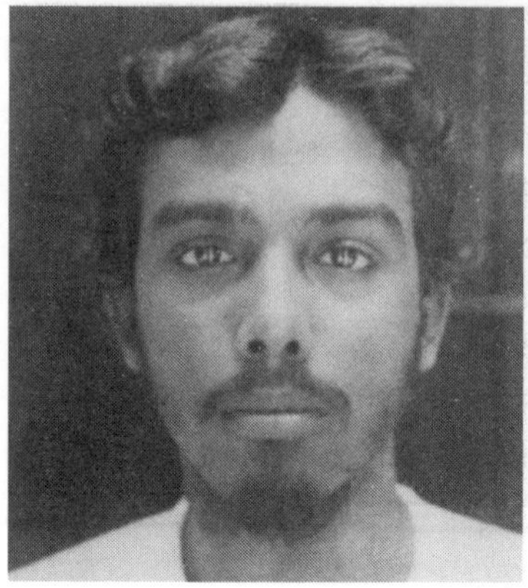

Indra Nath Nandy

Nikhileshwar Roy Moulik

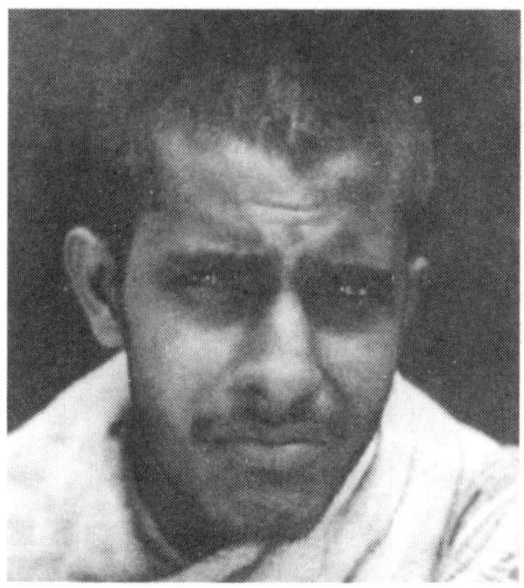

Bijoy Chandra Bhattacharjee

Bal Krishna Hari Kane

Din Dayal Bose

The courtroom where the Alipore Bomb Case trial was conducted is now a museum-cum-memorial

of politics. The whole of politics is an interference with personal liberty. Law is such an interference; protection is such an interference; the rule which makes the will of the majority prevail is such an interference.

The right to prevent such use of personal liberty as will injure the interests of the race, is the fundamental law of society. From this point of view the nation is only using its primary rights when it restrains the individual from buying or selling foreign goods.

It may be argued that peaceful compulsion is one thing, and violent compulsion, another. Social boycott may be justifiable, but not the burning or drowning of British goods. The latter method, we reply, is illegal and therefore may be inexpedient, but it is not morally unjustifiable.

The morality of the Kshatriya justifies violence in times of war, and boycott is a war. Nobody blames the Americans for throwing British tea into Boston harbour, nor can anybody blame a similar action in India on moral grounds.

It is reprehensible from the point of view of law, of social peace and order, not of political morality. It has been eschewed by us because it is unwise and because it carried the battle on to a ground where we are comparatively weak, from a ground where we are strong. Under other circumstances we might have followed the American

The seating arrangement, now a permanent display at the courtroom-museum

Another view of the courtroom-museum

precedent and if we had done so, historians and moralists would have applauded, not censured.

Justice and righteousness are the atmosphere of political morality, but the justice and righteousness of a fighter, not of the priest. Aggression is unjust only when unprovoked; violence, unrighteous when used wantonly or for unrighteous ends. It is a barren philosophy which applies a mechanical rule to all actions, or takes a word and tries to fit all human life into it.

The 'Sweets Letter'

The most important evidence was the following letter, also known as the 'Sweets Letter':

Bengal Camp,
27 December 1907

Dear Brother,
Now is the time. Please try and make them wait for our conference. We must have sweets all over India readymade for emergencies. I wait here for your answer.

Yours affectionately,
Barindra Kumar Ghose

Letter of Aurobindo Ghose to His Wife

30 August 1905

Dearest Mrinalini,
I have received your letter of 24 August. I am sorry to learn that the same affliction has fallen once more upon your parents. You have not written which of the boys has passed away from here. But then what can be done if the affliction comes. This is a world in which when you seek happiness you find grief in its heart, sorrow always clinging to joy ...

Now I will write the other thing of which I spoke before. I think you have understood by now that the man with whose fate yours has been linked is a man of a very unusual character. Mine is not the same field of action, the same purpose in life, the same mental attitude as that of the people of today in this country. I

> am in every respect different from them and out of the ordinary. Perhaps you know what ordinary men say of an extraordinary view, an extraordinary endeavour, an extraordinary ambition. To them it is madness; only, if the madman is successful in his work then he is called no longer a madman, but a great genius ... I have three madnesses. The first is that the accomplishments, genius, higher education and learning and wealth that God has given me are His .... .
>
> My second madness has only recently seized me. It is this: by whatever means I must have the direct vision of God .... .
>
> My third madness is that while others look upon their country as an inert piece of matter—a few meadows and fields, forests and hills and rivers—I look upon her as the mother. What would a son do if a demon sat on his mother's breast and started sucking her blood? Would he quietly sit down to his dinner, amuse himself with his wife and children, or would he rush out to deliver his mother? I know I have the strength to deliver this fallen race. It is not physical strength—I am not going to fight with sword or gun—but it is the strength of knowledge ... God sent me to earth to accomplish this great mission.
>
> Yours ...

Publication and Seizure of *Bartaman Ranoniti*

Literally meaning 'Modern War Strategy' or 'Present War Policy', *Bartaman Ranoniti* is a book on war preparation, funding, different attack tactics, strategies and their impact. Seized during the raids, it is believed to be an anonymous Bengali adaptation (sometimes also ascribed to Barin Ghose and Abinash Chandra Bhattacharji) of Ivan S. Bloch's famous book, *Modern Weapons and Modern War*, published in 1900.

On 4 March 1909, the Crown Counsel closed his evidence. The accused were then examined by the judge to explain the evidence against them. Almost all the accused declined to answer the questions put to them and merely stated that the lawyers on their behalf had their full instructions to argue and explain the evidence. Mr. Eardley Norton, Counsel for the King, then began his argument, which he finished on 20 March 1909. The Defence Counsel and pleaders then addressed the Court. Both sides argued the case at great length. Mr. Eardley Norton and Mr. Chittaranjan Das, the

Defence Counsel, argued the case with great legal acumen and scholarly erudition. Chittaranjan Das pleaded for Aurobindo Ghose for eight days. Their arguments went on till 13 April 1909. Das was indeed inspired, for he had the opportunity to defend a seer. The evidence against Aurobindo Ghose mostly consisted of his letters to his wife and his speeches and articles. Chittaranjan Das tried to establish that Aurobindo Ghose was a deeply religious and a God-inspired *Vedantist* whose patriotism and love for his countrymen were the basis of his politics. Chittaranjan Das referred to the evidence of several other witnesses and commented on them, after which he cogently summed them up:

> I ask you to disregard all that; the conspiracy is in my learned friend's imagination; I do not for a moment suggest that he does not believe it to be true; I don't suggest that he does not believe every word of what he has said and that he has no misgivings on the point.
>
> I wholly concede that he fully believed in the conspiracy which he has put forward before the Court and the only way I can explain that and the only suggestion that I can make is that he has been under the tutelage of the Police for a long time and the police has poisoned his mind during the last 10 months and no doubt he sincerely believed in it and put it forward before the court.

Chittaranjan Das went on to say:

> My submission to you is—I made it before and I do so again—that those papers and the writings and speeches are not legal evidence in the case at all; but if you do take them you find unmistakable indication that whatever may be Aurobindo's views, he is not guilty of the charges brought against him. I have placed before Your Honour the letter of 13 August 1905. I read to you the whole of the letter and commented on it, and I explained to you what the different thoughts in that letter are.

Chittaranjan Das then quotes Aurobindo Ghose:

> I say, as I have said in my statement, that ever since I came to Calcutta from Baroda, I never for one single moment deviated from the principles laid down in that letter. I have said I never took any part in politics. I have said in my written statement, whatever the nature of my activities, be they political, social or religious, that throughout the whole course of my activities, I never for one single moment deviated from the principle laid down in that letter of 13 August. The whole of my case before you is this. If it is suggested

Defence Counsel Chittaranjan Das who pleaded for Aurobindo Ghose for eight days

Eminent barrister, Mr. Eardley Norton, also known as the Lion of Madras Corporation

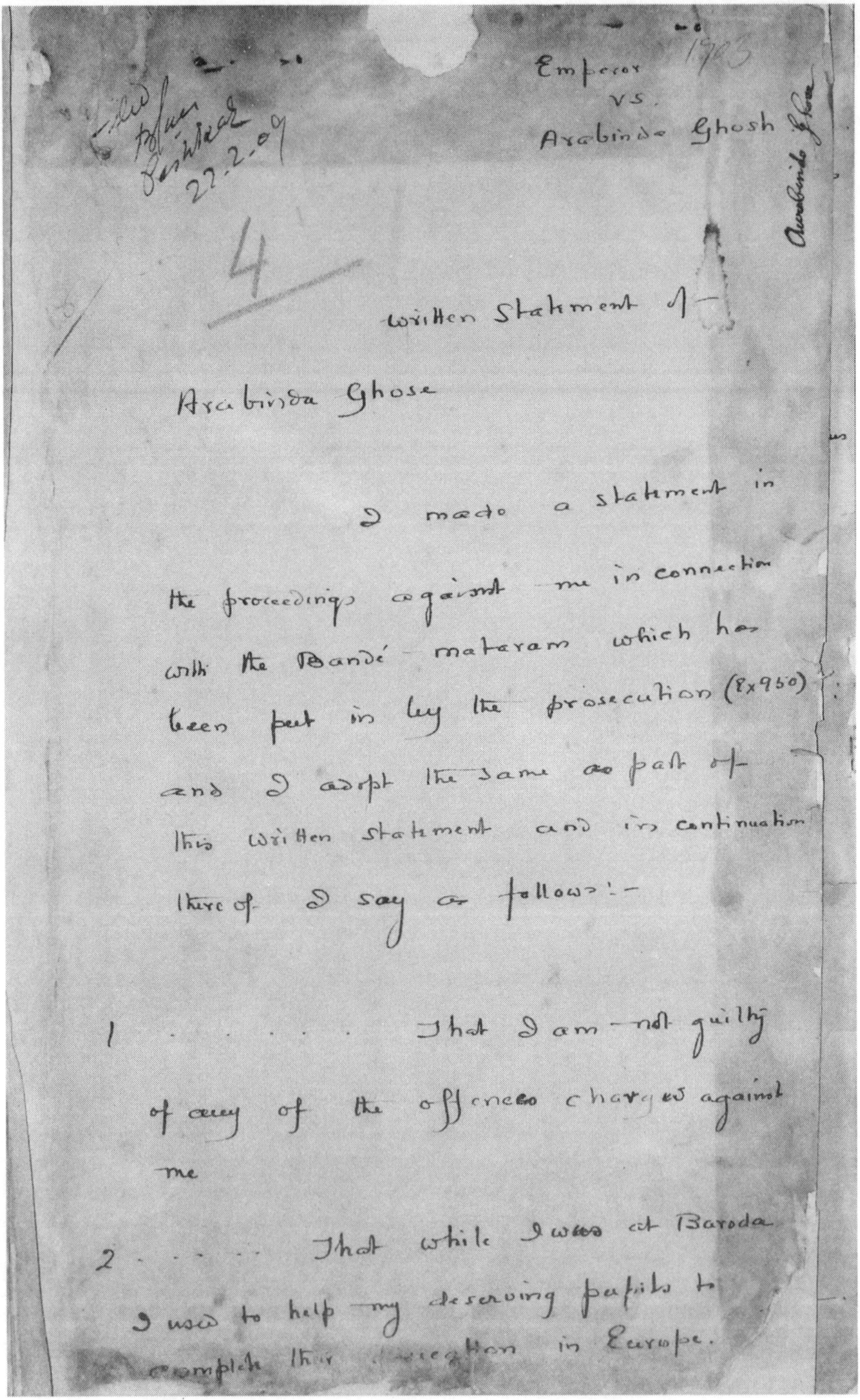

Emperor
vs.
Arabinda Ghosh

22.2.09

4

Written Statement of

Arabinda Ghose

I made a statement in connection with the proceedings against me in the Bandé Mataram which has been put in by the prosecution (Ex 950) and I adopt the same as part of this written statement and in continuation thereof I say as follows:-

1 . . . . . . That I am not guilty of any of the offences charged against me

2 . . . . That while I was at Baroda I used to help my deserving pupils to complete their education in Europe.

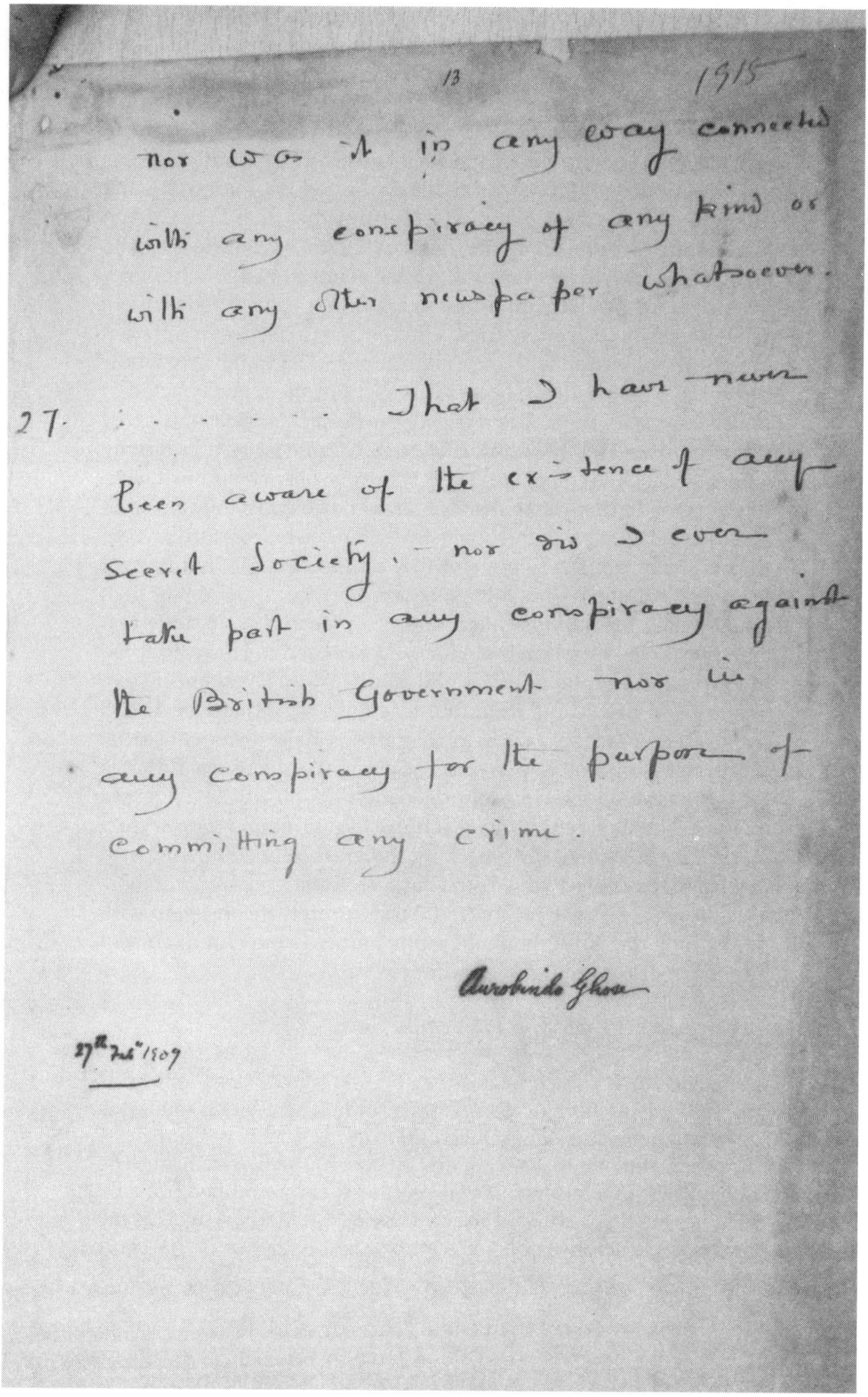

13 1515

nor was it in any way connected with any conspiracy of any kind or with any other newspaper whatsoever.

27. . . . . . . That I have never been aware of the existence of any secret society, nor did I ever take part in any conspiracy against the British Government nor in any conspiracy for the purpose of committing any crime.

Aurobindo Ghose

27th Feb 1909

An extract of Aurobindo Ghose's statement

> that I preached the ideal of freedom to my country, which is against the law, I plead guilty to the charge. If that is the law here, I say I have done that and I request you to convict me. But do not impute to me crimes that I am not guilty of; deeds against which my whole nature revolts, and which, having regard to my mental capacity are something, which could never have been perpetrated by me. If it is an offence to preach the ideal of freedom, I admit having done it—I have never disputed it. It is for that, that I have given up all the prospects of my life. It is for that, that I came to Calcutta to live for it and to labour for it. It has been the one thought of my waking hours, the dream of my sleep. If that is my offence, there is no necessity to bring witness into the box to depose to different things in connection with that. Here am I and I admit it. My whole submission before the Court is this. Let not the scene enacted in connection with the sedition trial of the *Bande Mataram* be enacted over again, and let the whole trial go into a side issue. If that is my offence let it be so stated and I am cheerful to bear any punishment. It pains me to think that crimes I could never have thought of or deeds repellent to me, and against which my whole nature revolts, should be attributed to me and that on the strength, not only of evidence on which the slightest reliance breathe only of that high ideal which I felt I was called upon to preach. I have done that and there is no question that I have ever denied it. I have adopted the principles of the political philosophy of the West and I have assimilated that to the immortal teachings of Vedantism. I felt I was called upon to preach to my country to make them realise that India had a mission to perform in the comity of nations. If that is my fault you can chain me, imprison me, but you will never get out of me a denial of that charge. I venture to submit under no section of the law do I come for preaching the ideal of freedom and with regard to the deeds with which I have been charged, I submit there is no evidence on the record and it is absolutely inconsistent with everything that I taught, that I wrote and with every tendency of my mind discovered in the evidence.

A truly inspired Chittaranjan Das appealed:

> Long after this controversy is hushed in silence, long after this turmoil, this agitation ceases, long after he (Aurobindo Ghose) is dead and gone, he will be looked upon as the poet of patriotism, as the prophet of nationalism and the lover of humanity. Long after he is dead and gone his words will be echoed and re-echoed not only in India, but across distant seas and lands. Therefore I say that the man in his position is not only standing before the bar of this court but before the bar of the High Court of history.

He concluded his address with the following words:

> And now gentlemen, you have heard that last of the speeches on behalf of the defence. So far as this historic trial is concerned—the

> first of its kind in India—what remains now is for you, Gentlemen Assessors, to give your opinions and for His Honour the Judge to deliver his judgement. I have the unique honour and opportunity, Sir, of appearing before you in two of the longest trials over which you have presided here in Alipore—perhaps the longest in your Honour's experience as a Judge in this country. In the other case—K.E.V. Habib and others—all the accused persons were acquitted by your Honour. I do not know, neither can I anticipate, what the result of this trial will be but I have not the least doubt that justice will be vindicated. The task of finding out the really relevant pieces of evidence from the vast mass of irrelevant evidence put in this case is indeed Herculean. Ridiculed by a reptile press, looked on with suspicion by the prying police, hampered in our work by the want of facilities for proper instructions, weighed down with the enormity of accumulated prejudice, we have toiled on for months actuated only by the highest and the noblest motives, which inspire the profession—holding aloft the glorious tradition for which the Bar stands, to help justice and to vindicate innocence— cheered in our labours by the only redeeming feature in the case, the uniform courtesy we have received from the Bench. To think that all the 36 persons arraigned at the dock behind us are guilty of a conspiracy to wage war against the King is outrageous. I have no doubt, Sir, that you will decide this case as an English Judge would do—for justice is the bulwark of the state. British rule in India is broad-based upon the hearts and affections of the people, not because of its brave Army or invincible Navy—but on account of its strict and impartial administration of justice wherein its real strength lies. Long after the dust of controversy and racial feeling that have been raised over this unfortunate case will be forgotten and when history alone will remain to bear evidence to this strange episode and to write with its unerring hand on the tablet of time its just and eternal verdict—the one fact, which people will never forget and will cherish with pride and satisfaction, will be that there was a British Judge who kept himself cool, whose judgement was not warped by prejudices and predilections, who held the scales even and did justice for the sake of justice.

The Court was thus engaged till 13 April 1909. On 14 April the opinion of the assessors was taken ... And Charles Porten Beachcroft delivered his judgement on 6 May 1909.

The Judgement of C.P. Beachcroft

While delivering the judgement, the Judge, Mr. C.P. Beachcroft, observed that the case had lasted much longer than it ought to have either on account of its importance or the novelty of the charges. For this, he believed that both sides were to be blamed for the prosecution introduced incidents and numerous evidences, which did not have much bearing on the case. He further realised that due to a lack of time, the examination of many of those documents had not been done. However, on the other side, the cross-examination was also more detailed than was necessary. Nevertheless, the judge agreed that the case, as he understood it, had caused him considerable anxiety on account of its importance, its difficulty, and partly also on account of the circumstances in which it was launched. While examining the documents, Beachcroft accepted that that the scrutiny of the evidences had created a feeling of prejudice in the minds of the public before whom one of the accused had for some time been a conspicuous figure.

Delivering the judgement, Beachcroft dealt with the legal objections taken to the jurisdiction of the court to try the accused. He said:

> First, Mr. Das argued that the accused had a right to be tried by the jury, and that the Criminal Procedure Code, so far as it provides for trials with the aid of assessors, is *ultra vires*. I declined to hear Mr. Das, as an exactly similar point was raised a short time ago before the Special Branch of the High Court and rejected.
>
> The next point was that Mr. Birley had no jurisdiction to commit the case, and that the only Magistrate having jurisdiction was the Chief Presidency Magistrate. A similar point was raised at the beginning of the hearing but in the arguments at the end an additional point

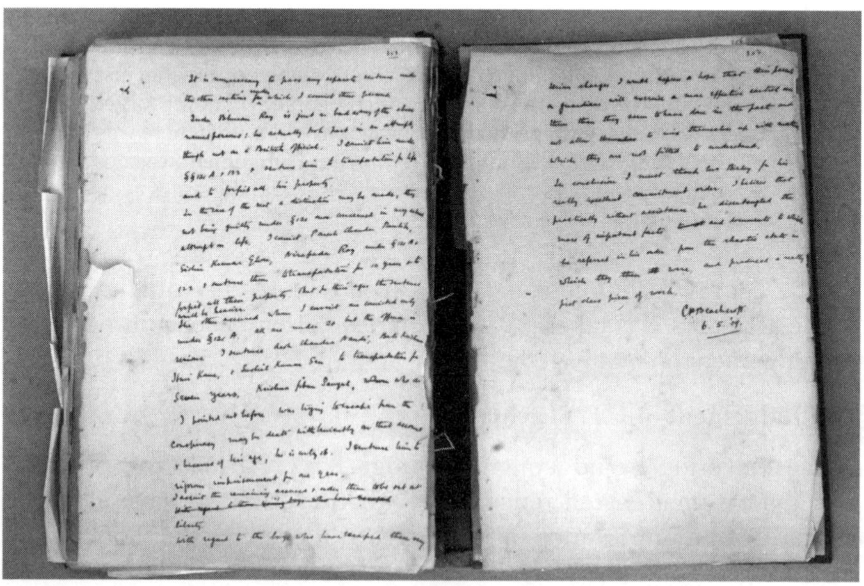

A section of the landmark judgement delivered by C.P. Beachcroft

> was taken, which was not taken at the beginning, as it should have been, for it might have made a very great difference: that objection was taken to Mr. Birley's jurisdiction when he first began the inquiry; for if objection was taken, the Section 532, CPC, would not cure the defect. But I do not see how the fact that Mr. Thornhill issued warrants can affect Mr. Birley's jurisdiction: Mr. Birley could only take cognisance on complaints made under Section 196 CPC, and when the sanction of the government was given the complaint was made to Mr. Birley who had local jurisdiction.

Giving his views on the opinion of the assessors, Beachcroft continued:

> One of them speaks of this conspiracy as a childish conspiracy. He seems to have utterly failed to realise the significance and danger of it or the extent to which it had spread. The assessors evidently dislike the idea of conspiracy; while both find that certain persons collected arms in circumstances that amount to an offence under Section 122; one of them thinks that the collections were made by persons independently of each other. In fact, the offence under Section 122 is more serious than that under Section 121A, involving as it does, forfeiture of all offenders' property as a compulsory sentence.
>
> I take Section 121A to be an amplification of what is meant by waging war in Section 121. But to say that the offence of waging war is only completed with the formation of battle array and the commencement of hostilities is to claim a meaning for those words which, to my mind, is far too narrow. It might have been a correct interpretation in the Middle Ages, but as was pointed out by the judges in the case of Rex vs. Gallaker the offence under Section 121 was the most serious in the Penal Code except that of murder by a life-convict; and the Criminal Procedure Code provided that where a person was convicted of an offence for which capital sentence was provided as a punishment, reasons must be given if such a sentence was not passed.
>
> The attempt, however, on Mr. Kingsford stands on a different footing. It is true that Mr. Kingsford had earned the hatred of the conspirators for his convicting some of the persons instrumental in spreading revolutionary ideas, and their conviction was a blow to the methods of the conspirators.
>
> But here there is no question of a line of policy pursued by one of the King's Ministers. His acts convicting the accused were individual acts of a judicial nature. At the time of the attempt he had ceased to be Chief Presidency Magistrate, so was no longer in a position to check the work of the conspiracy by sentencing those who preached revolution. In his case the act looks more like an act of revenge than one in furtherance of the conspiracy.

There is another point of view that might be taken. It might be said that, as an act of terrorism, it was in pursuance of the conspiracy. But to convert a conspiracy into an abetment, the overt act must be not only in pursuance of the conspiracy but in order to the doing of the thing, that is, in their case to the doing of one of the things, mentioned in Section 121A.

Then, if it is to apply to any, it must clearly be to the first act contemplated in Section 121A, that is, to commit one of the offences, under Section 121. It cannot be said that to kill Mr. Kingsford was in order to the waging of war. I am therefore of the opinion that the attempt on Mr. Kingsford was not such as to convert the conspiracy into abetment of waging war.

It follows then that while all of the persons whom I have found to be members of the conspiracy are guilty under Section 121A, only those will be guilty under Section 121, who joined the conspiracy before the 5 December, the last day on which an attempt was made on the Lieutenant Governor. And those, the evidence that I have already set out, shows to be Barin, Upen, Ullaskar, Bibhuti, Hrishikesh, Biren Sen (the date in the book of the explosive fixes it in his case), Sudhir, Indra Nath, Abinash, Sailendra and Hem Chandra Das. The absence of the last named from India till the beginning of 1908 seems to suggest that he could not have belonged to the conspiracy before that, but Barin's confession shows that his object in going to Paris was also to learn explosives as well as mechanics, and the fact that he was in touch with the conspiracy immediately on his return and the mention, in his letter, of the work that he had to do supports Barin's statement. Of the above-named Barin, Ullaskar, Bibhuti are guilty of waging war, as they were actually concerned in specific attempts; the others are guilty of abetment of waging war. Section 122 is very wide in its terms. It includes not merely the collection of arms and ammunition, but preparation of any sort, with the intention of waging war or of being prepared to wage war. It seems to contemplate a stage intermediate between the stages covered by Sections 121A and 121.

The accused, whom the evidence establishes to have committed the offence under this Section, are Barin, Upen, Ullaskar, Indu Bhushan, Bibhuti, Hem Chandra Das, Paresh, Sishir, Hrishikesh, Nirapodo, Biren Sen, Indra Nath, Sudhir and Sailendra. The liability of the last two named under the Section is established by their presence at Sils' Lodge.

The result is that, agreeing with both assessors, I find the accused Barindra Kumar Ghose, Indu Bhusan Rai, Ullaskar Dutt, Upendra Nath Banerjee, Bibhuti Bhusan Sarkar, Hem Chandra Das, Hrishikesh Kanjilal guilty under Section 122, IPC and, agreeing with one and disagreeing with one, I find Paresh Chandra Moulik and Sudhir Kumar Ghose guilty under Section 122, IPC.

Disagreeing with both, I find the following guilty under Sections 121 and 121A—Barindra Kumar Ghose, Upendra Nath Banerjee, Ullaskar Dutt, Bibhuti Bhushan Sarkar, Hrishikesh, Hem Chandra Das, Birendra Chandra Sen, Sudhir Kumar Sarkar, Indra Nath Nandy, Abinash Chandra Bhattacharjee, Sailendra Nath Bose and the following guilty under Section 121A—Indu Bhusan Rai, Paresh Chandra Moulik, Sishir Kumar Ghose, Krishna Jiban Sanyal, Asoke Chandra Nandy, Bal Krishna Hari Kane, Sushil Kumar Sen, Nirapodo Rai and the following guilty under Section 122— Nirapodo Rai, Birendra Chandra Sen, Sudhir Kumar Sarkar, Indra Nath Nandy and Sailendra Nath Bose. Agreeing with both assessors, I find the following not guilty under Section 121—Indu Bhusan, Paresh, Sishir, Krishna Jiban, Nirapodo, Asoke, Kane, Sushil and the following not guilty under Section 122—Krishna Jiban, Asoke, Kane, Sushil, Abinash.

Agreeing with both, I find Naren Bakshi, Sailendra Kumar Sen, Nalini Kanti Gupta, Purna Chandra Sen, Bijoy Kumar Nag, Kunja Lall Shaha, Hemendra Nath Ghose, Dharni Nath Gupta, Nogendra Nath Gupta, Birendra Nath Ghose; Bijoy Bhattacharji, Hem Chandra Sen, Provash Chandra Deb, Dindayal Bose, Nikhileshwar Roy Maulik, Debabrata Bose, Aurobindo Ghose not guilty under Sections 121, 121A and 122, and all accused persons not guilty under Section 123.

Some extracts from Beachcroft's judgement regarding Aurobindo Ghose:

- I now come to the case of Aurobindo Ghose, the most important accused in the case. He is the accused, whom more than any other the prosecution are anxious to have convicted and but for his presence in the dock there is no doubt that the case would have been finished long ago. It is partly for that reason that I have left his case till last of all and partly because the case against him depends to a very great extent, in fact almost entirely, upon association with other accused persons.
- Before dealing with the evidence against him I shall put as shortly as possible the ideal which his Counsel claims that he has always set before himself. It is the case for the prosecution as well as for the defence that he is of a very religious nature, in fact the Counsel for the Crown takes the line that his religious ideas combined with a desire for independence for India turned him into a fanatic.
- His Counsel argues that he is a Vedantist and that he has applied the doctrines of Vedantism to mould his political views; that as the doctrine of Vedantism applied to the individual is to look for the godhead within oneself and so

realise what is best within oneself, so in the case of a nation, it can only grow by realising what is best within itself, that no foreigner can give it that salvation, which it can only attain by methods indigenous to the country. His doctrines are not those of passive resistance, but of the realisation of salvation by suffering. If the law is unjust don't obey it, and take the consequences. Do not be violent, but if the law is unjust, you are not bound morally to obey it; refuse to obey it and suffer. He has been saying to the people: You are not cowards, believe in yourselves and attain salvation, not by assistance from outside, but through yourselves. And this Mr. Das says is the key of his case ... .

- He points out (referring to Aurobindo's correspondence with his wife) that his views and mental attitude are different from those of the people of this country and goes on to say that an extraordinary man is generally looked upon as either great or mad: and then says that he had got three ideas, which he characterises as mad, in what is doubtless a play on the word used in the earlier part of the letter. The first idea is that gifts given by God should be used in the service of God and he refers more particularly to their use in works of charity. The second idea is that he is realising the teachings of Hindu religion and feeling God within himself. The third idea is the one in which occur the passages on which the prosecution lays stress: "I know I have the strength to deliver this fallen nation. I may not have bodily strength, but I am not going to fight with sword or gun but with the power of knowledge."

  In the last paragraph but one of the letter, he speaks of deliverance of the country. And in the last paragraph he speaks of all this as a secret. Mr. Das argues that the third idea is drawn from Vedantism. The idea is that the whole world is divinity: if you can't see that, it is *maya*, or illusion. The country should not be regarded as so many rivers, fields, etc., but as a manifestation of the divinity. And if that be the true view of the passage it is only natural that he should speak of removing anything which stands in the way of the ideal ... .

  If we start with the knowledge that the writer of this letter is a conspirator we can find passages in it that are suspicious, viewing it in an unprejudiced way there is nothing in it that really calls for explanation ... .

- There are passages in it (referring to the article, 'The Morality of Boycott') which taken by themselves certainly indicate support of the use of violent methods and suggest that his line was that revealed by this conspiracy, first inspire your followers with religious enthusiasm and then get them to take up arms ... .

The argument of the whole article shortly is this: "To drive out that which is evil violence is justifiable. We don't hate the English, but we object to their exploiting the country, for the interests of the two nations must be different: and we can stop that exploitation by boycott. Boycott is not morally wrong for the ends at which it aims are the interests of the people. And that being so we should be morally justified in using force, if we were strong enough to do so."

As a mere piece of philosophic writing there is no special harm in this. The danger is the state of feeling in the country at the time and the suggestion that violence is justifiable if the nation wishes for a particular thing: the fact that in the circumstances the nation should not use violence is relegated to the background, equally so the questions who is to decide what are the best interests of the nation. It is left for the reader to come to the conclusion that those who can make their voices heard most are to decide what are the interests of the nation and impose on the inarticulate masses a tyranny far worse than that which they themselves condemn.

- I should hesitate before saying that his complicity in the conspiracy can be considered established on these facts. In his favour we have the fact that he has in the columns of *Bande Mataram* deprecated violence: there is such an article dated 28 May 1907..... His connection with the conspiracy can only be considered established if we find that while writing one thing he has been doing another.

Of course it is possible that a man might join a conspiracy to deprive the King of the sovereignty of British India, in which his share would be to preach discontent and that he might be entirely ignorant of that branch of the conspiracy which commenced collection of arms and ammunition. It is possible that Aurobindo may have been in that position in this case, but in such a case it must be clearly shown that his preachings were part of such a conspiracy, and in the present case it would be difficult to do that without showing some connection with the part which the garden plays in the case. Considering the circumstances of India it may be dangerous for a man to publish doctrines inconsistent with the existing order of things, in certain circumstances it might justify a charge of sedition. Whether such a charge could be laid at Aurobindo's door does not now concern me. The point is whether his writings and speeches, which in themselves seem to advocate nothing more than the regeneration of his country, taken with the facts proved against him in this case are sufficient to show that he was a member of the conspiracy. And taking all the evidence together I am of the opinion that it falls short of such proof as would justify me in finding him guilty of so serious a charge.

The Sentences

- Accused Barindra Kumar Ghose (brother of Aurobindo Ghose) and Ullaskar Dutt were sentenced to be hanged under Sections 121, 121A and 122 IPC.
- Accused Hem Chandra Das, Upendra Nath Banerjee, Bibhuti Bhusan Sarkar, Hrishikesh Kanjilal, Birendra Chandra Sen, Sudhir Kumar Ghose, Indra Nath Nandy, Abinash Chandra Bhattacharji, Sailendra Bose and Indu Bhusan Rai were sentenced to be transported for life under Sections 121 and 122.
- Paresh Moulik, Sishir Kumar Ghose, Nirapodo Rai were sentenced to transportation for 10 years under Sections 121 and 122.

  The properties of all the accused were also forfeited to the government.
- Ashok Chandra Nandy, Bal Krishna Hari Kane, Sushil Kumar Sen were sentenced to transportation for seven years.
- Krishna Jibon Sanyal was sentenced to one year's rigorous imprisonment.

The other accused—Nalini Kanti Gupta, Sachindra Kumar Sen, Kunja Lall Saha, Bijoy Kumar Nag, Narendra Nath Bakshi, Purna Chandra Sen, Hemendra Nath Ghose, Dindayal Bose, Birendra Nath Ghose, Dharani Nath Gupta, Nogendra Nath Gupta, Hem Chandra Sen, Debabrata Bose, Nikhileshwar Roy Moulik, Bijoy Chandra Bhattacharjee Provash Chandra Deb and Aurobindo Ghose—were acquitted.

At the end of the judgement, Beachcroft thanked Mr. Birley (District Magistrate, 24 Parganas) for his excellent committal order. He believed that Birley had extracted a mass of important facts and documents from the chaotic state in which they then were and produced "a really first class piece of work". Beachcroft noted that the question of sentence had also caused him much anxiety because only one of the accused whom he found guilty was over 30; some had barely crossed 20 … . "For many of them one could not help being sorry, feeling that they were young and impressionable, and could easily be motivated and influenced by those persons, who, whether they called themselves moderates, or whether having the courage of convictions they called themselves extremists, were alike in this… ."

Chapter Four

The Aftermath and Beyond

There were many who thought that the judgement in the Alipore Bomb Case was a setback for the revolutionary groups. They couldn't have been more incorrect because instead of pushing them back, the judgement infused more energy, excitement and spirit of independence in their efforts as well as ideologies. The bomb hurled by Khudiram had become an exemplary inspirational act. The case that followed also helped to create many more revolutionary icons. The next decade was witness to the revolutionary acts of many secret societies as they continued their effort to eliminate high-ranking British officials, demoralise the British and ultimately force them to quit India.

The Prosecution of Lokmanya Bal Gangadhar Tilak

The Muzaffarpur bombing got praise from none other than the famous nationalist leader Lokmanya Bal Gangadhar Tilak who was known for his fiery writings and revolutionary speeches. In his explicitly bold Marathi weekly, *Kesari*, Tilak wrote a series of articles, including 'The Country's Misfortune,' in which he stated that the murders committed by the revolutionaries of Bengal had been in retaliation against the oppression that had been heaped upon them by the British. He also drew attention to the fact that the cause of the murders was not hatred between individuals, private quarrels or disputes. He wrote that the motive was much higher. He also said that while pistols and muskets were old weapons, it was the bomb that was the latest discovery of the Western scientist ... It was Western science itself that had created new guns, new muskets and new ammunition, and now it was the Westerner's science again that had created the bomb.

Tilak added that while the bomb by itself was not capable of destroying the military strength of a government or crippling the power of an army, the Muzaffarpur bombing had not only succeeded in attracting the government's attention to the disorder that prevailed but had also dented the military pride of the British.

Famous nationalist leader Lokmanya Bal Gangadhar Tilak

Writings like these were too fiery for the British. To them, it was more than seditious enough to warrant the arrest of Tilak. Such an outspoken man had to be separated from his people. Tilak was arrested and prosecuted under Sections 124A and 153A. A long-drawn legal battle took place in the Court before Justice Davar. Defending himself, Tilak prepared a masterly defence that is today considered a document of great historical importance. At the end, the nine-member jury found him guilty by a verdict of seven to two. Tilak was sentenced to transportation for six years to the dreaded prisons of Mandalay in Burma and fined Rs. 1,000. When asked by Judge Davar if he had anything more to say, he spoke the memorable lines that are inscribed in stone at the entrance to the courtroom in which he was tried at the High Court of Bombay:

> All I wish to say is that in spite of the verdict of the jury, I maintain that I am innocent. There are higher powers that rule the destiny of things and it may be the will of providence that the cause I represent may prosper more by my suffering than by my remaining free.

The Appeal in the High Court of Judicature at Fort William

After the Sessions Court judgement was delivered in the Alipore Bomb Conspiracy Case, the accused who had been convicted were initially in a dilemma as to whether to appeal in the High Court or not. The two main accused—Ullaskar Dutt and Barindra Kumar Ghose—who had been sentenced to be hanged, finally filed their appeal in the High Court of Judicature at Fort William in Bengal on 13 May 1909 (subsequently followed by the other accused). Sarat Chandra Sen, the Counsel for the accused, filed their appeal before the Chief Justice, Hon'ble Sir Lawrence Hugh Jenkins, Kt. K.C.I.E. and his companion Judges of the High Court. The convicted accused stated in their petitions:

- That they were arrested on 2 May 1908 and placed on trial before Mr. L. Birley (officiating District Magistrate of 24 Parganas) who, after a preliminary enquiry on 19 August and 2 September 1908, had committed the petitioners to take their trial, which commenced on 19 October 1908 with the aid of two assessors who on 14 April 1909 found the accused guilty only under Section 122 of the Indian Penal Code.

- That on 6 May 1909, the petitioners were then convicted under Sections 121, 121A and 122 IPC by Mr. C.P. Beachcroft, Additional Sessions Judge. Barindra Kumar Ghose and Ullaskar Dutt were sentenced to be hanged.
- That being aggrieved by the said order of conviction and the sentence, the petitioners were now referring the appeal to the Hon'ble High Court of Judicature on the following, among other, grounds:

1. That neither the Court of the Committing Magistrate nor the Court of Sessions had any jurisdiction to inquire into or try the offences charged inasmuch as there was no complaint such as is contemplated by Section 136 of the Criminal Procedure.
2. That the trial was bad because of the misjoinder of persons and charges.
3. That the case of some of the accused being in the seisin of the Chief Presidency Magistrate, the Committing Magistrate had no jurisdiction to inquire into their cases nor had the Sessions Court any jurisdiction to try the case.
4. That the alleged confessions put in by the prosecution were inadmissible documents and the procedure adopted was irregular.
5. That on the facts and circumstances of the case, the accused should be acquitted.
6. That petitioner No. 2 (Barindra Kumar Ghose), being a European British subject, the learned Sessions Judge could not sentence him to more than a year's imprisonment.
7. That in any event the sentence given was too severe.

Submitting their petitions, the petitioners appealed to the High Court to send for the records of the case, and after hearing the petitioners' Counsel to set aside the convictions and the sentence, or pass such other order or orders as may seem fit and proper.

On 9 August, the Chief Justice, Sir Lawrence Hugh Jenkins and Justice H.W.C. Carnduff (who tried the case of Khudiram Bose) commenced hearing the appeal. The arguments continued till 12 October 1909. Chief Justice Jenkins and Justice Carnduff delivered separate judgements.

From the Judgement of Chief Justice Sir Lawrence Hugh Jenkins:

The result then is that the convictions and sentences against all the accused under Sections 121 and 122 must be set aside but, as against Barindra Kumar Ghose, Ullaskar Dutt, Upendra Nath Banerjee, Indu Bhushan Rai, Bibhuti Bhushan Sarkar, Hrishikesh Kanjilal, Sudhir Kumar Sarkar, Hem Chandra Das, Paresh Chandra Moulik, Sisir Kumar Ghose, Nirapodo Rai and Abinash Chandra Bhattacharji, the convictions under Section 121A of the Indian Penal Code should (in my opinion) be confirmed.

The question of punishment is one of considerable difficulty. Those who have been convicted are not ordinary criminals. They are for the most part men of education, of strong religious instincts and in some cases of considerable force of character. At the same time they have been convicted of one of the most serious offences against the King and the punishment conspired to wage war against the King and the punishment must be in proportion to the gravity of the offence. For the purpose of punishment Barindra Kumar Ghose, Ullaskar Dutt, Upendra Nath Banerjee and Hem Chandra Das may properly be grouped together, for they were the leaders of the society and Ullaskar Dutt and Hem Chandra Das actually manufactured the bombs that were used. We sentence each of them to transportation for life. The next class includes Bibhuti Bhushan Sarkar, Hrishikesh Kanjilal and Indu Bhushan Rai, whose prominence in the society is shown by the part they took in one or other of the attempted outrages disclosed by the evidence in the case. We sentence each of them to transportation for a term of 10 years.

We sentence each of the following, that is, Sudhir Kumar Sarkar, Paresh Chandra Moulik, Abinash Chandra Bhattacharji to transportation for a term of seven years. We sentence Sisir Kumar Ghose and Nirapodo Rai, respectively, to five years rigorous imprisonment.

Mr. Justice Carnduff and I are divided in opinion as to the conviction of Krishna Jiban Sanyal, Sushil Kumar Sen, Birendra Chandra Sen, Sailendra Nath Bose and Indra Nath Nandi. So the case, with our opinions thereon, must be laid before another Judge of the Court as provided in Section 429 of the Criminal Procedure Code.

Again I wish to express my sense of obligation to all those who have assisted in this difficult and complex enquiry. Though against several of the accused the convictions under Section 121A of the Indian Penal Code have been upheld; it is a satisfaction to feel that those accused have been represented before us by Counsel and pleaders who have spared no effort of industry on their behalf, and have brought to our notice everything that could be legitimately argued for their clients' advantage: and I desire in particular to place on record my high appreciation of the manner in which the case was presented to this Court by their leading advocate, Mr. C.R. Das.

From the Judgement of Justice H.W.C. Carnduff:

I agree with most, but unfortunately not with all, of the conclusions arrived at by My Lord the Chief Justice on this appeal. Our difference of opinion is, in effect, limited to the question whether the guilt of a few of the appellants has been proved or not. But there are some remarks which I feel called upon to make, as briefly as may be, on my own account, both on the case as it presents itself to me as a whole, and on certain points connected with it, although we are in substantial agreement regarding them.

These remarks I would adopt and apply *mutatis mutandis*, to Mr. Das's contention in this case. Moreover, trial by jury as known to the common law of England—that is to say, trial by the unanimous voice of 12 of one's peers—is unknown in India; and it seemed to Mr. Justice Harrington, Mr. Justice Mookerjee and myself last March, as it seems to me today, that it is too late now to question the validity of every law regulating criminal procedure that has been enacted in this country under the Statutes of 1833 and 1861, and the legality of every trial held whether by jury or with the aid of assessors in the Muffassil, or by jury before the Supreme or the High Court, during the last 76 years at least.

Secondly, as regards the question of waiver, I agree in thinking it settled by authority that a European British subject can relinquish his right to be tried as such, and that the appellant Barindra Kumar Ghose did so. And I would add that he seems to have acted deliberately and after the fullest warning and explanation of the position.

And, thirdly, I agree in considering that the expression 'wages war', which is used in Section 121 of the Indian Penal Code, must be construed in its ordinary sense as a phrase in common use in the English language and that it is impossible to hold that any of the overt acts alleged in this case amount to the offence provided for by that section. The charge thereunder, therefore, fails on the merits and the death sentences passed on Barindra Kumar Ghose and Ullaskar Dutt cannot be confirmed. I also think that there was no valid authority for the prosecution of the first batch of the accused on that charge, and I would endorse all the principles laid down by the learned Chief Justice in this connection but, as his Lordship has indicated, a decision on the point is not, in the view which we take of the offence concerned, essential.

It remains for me now only to refer to the cases of the appellants individually. As regards (1) Barindra Kumar Ghose, (2) Ullaskar Dutt, (3) Upendra Nath Banerjee, (4) Hem Chandra Das, (5) Bibhuti Bhusan Sarkar, (6) Hrishikesh Kanjilal, (7) Indu Bhushan Rai, (8) Abinash Chandra Bhattacharji, (9) Nirapodo Rai, (10) Sisir Kumar Ghose, (11) Paresh Chandra Moulik and (12) Sudhir Kumar Sarkar, I agree throughout with the learned Chief Justice, both in respect of the offences charged and in respect of the reduction of some of the sentences proposed, now that the conviction for waging war, for which the minimum penalty fixed by law is transportation for life, has been ruled out. And as to (13) Bal Krishna Hari Kane, I also concur in thinking that there is room for considerable doubt, to the benefit of which he is of course entitled. But as regards the remaining five, namely, Sushil Kumar Sen, Birendra Chandra Sen, Krishna Jiban Sanyal, Sailendra Nath Bose and Indra Nath Nandy, I regret that, for reasons which I have recorded separately, I cannot bring myself into agreement with my Lord. His Lordship then gave his reasons for differing in the case of these five appellants. In conclusion, I venture expressly to associate myself with the remarks made by his Lordship as to the assistance which we have received from both sides, and the manner in which the case for the appellants has been laid before us.

The Alipore Bomb Conspiracy Case became the cynosure of the nationalist movement in its time. It became the eye of the whirlpool and as we look back on history, we can see that it was a harbinger of things to come. A potent drop in the ocean of impassioned nationalist zeal, it sent out powerful ripples in many directions. Some of these ripples were very violent. Its first targets were the officials who had either sided or sympathised with the British Government at any stage of the arrests and the trials. Many sympathisers were killed during and after the trial in different parts of Bengal and also in other parts of the country. The following incidents are specifically related to the Alipore Bomb Case:

- Nandlal Banerjee, the police inspector who had been instrumental in the arrest of Prafulla Chaki, was shot dead in Serpentine Lane, Calcutta, on 9 November 1908.
- Ashutosh Biswas, who had acted as the official prosecutor in the Alipore Bomb Conspiracy Case and in the case of the murder of Narendra Nath Gossain (the revolutionary-turned-government approver killed by Kanai Lal Dutta and Satyendra Nath Bose) was assassinated by Charu Charan Bose while

leaving the Suburban Police Court, at Jorabagan in Calcutta. The assassination highlighted the organisational strength and strategic intelligence developed by the secret societies.

- Shamsul Alam, Deputy Superintendent of Police, was shot dead in the corridors of the Calcutta High Court on 24 January 1910, where he was attending the hearing of the appeal of the accused.

Many other significant events had occurred right after the first arrests were made at Maniktola in May 1908. Bombs were thrown at various places and into railway carriages, near Calcutta. This included the failed attempt on 15 May 1908 to kill Government Prosecutor, Mr. Hume, by throwing a bomb into the train in which he was travelling. Hume escaped because he wasn't in the bombed carriage.

Preventive Measures

The policing of revolutionary activities and thoughts were strengthened through the enactment of the Prevention of Seditious Meetings Act of 1907 that authorised the government to prohibit public meetings within areas designated as 'proclaimed'.

The Press Act of 1908 was also layered with harsher and more drastic sentences to control seditious writings. Another important preventive measure taken by the British was the passing of the Criminal Law Amendment Act XIV on 11 December 1908.

The statute made provisions for offences and offenders to be tried after an abridged form of preliminary investigation by a special bench of the three High Court Judges—without either assessors or a jury. It also strengthened the Governor General-in-Council's powers to declare some types of associations as unlawful. Under this enactment, the Dacca Anushilan Samiti, Sadesh Bandhav Samiti of Bakarganj, Brati Samiti of Faridpur, Suhrid Samiti and Sadhana Samiti of Mymensingh—all based in Eastern Bengal—were declared illegal in January 1908.

Constitutional Reforms

In November 1905, Lord Minto succeeded Lord Curzon as the new British Governor-General and Viceroy of India. As he took over the reins of the great Bangla Divide bequeathed by his predecessor, he made no attempts to deviate from the path that he had inherited. In fact, the entire build-up of revolutionary activity in Bengal and the whole course of the Alipore

Bomb Conspiracy Case actually unfolded during Lord Minto's tenure from November 1905 to November 1910. In one of his letters to Lord Morley, the Secretary of State for India, Lord Minto wrote:

> The Raj will not disappear in India as long as the British race remains what it is, because we shall fight for the Raj as hard as we have ever fought if it comes to fighting, and we shall win as we have always done. My great object is that it shall not come to that.

While his crackdown on revolutionary terrorism continued, Minto tried to assuage the sentiments of the *bhadralok*s of Bengal, the Muslims, as well as the loyalists in the upper segments of society through another masterstroke of politics that was conciliatory at one level and divisive at another. This was the strategic enlargement of the Legislative Councils and the introduction of the electoral principle through the Government of India Act of 1909. Specific classes of Indians could now be 'elected' and not just nominated to the Councils.

The Act also introduced separate electorates for Muslims, where only Muslims could stand for elections and cast votes. The Morley-Minto Reforms, as they came to be known (named after their perpetuators Lord Minto and Lord Morley) proved to be a landmark in the shaping of future national and international sub-continental politics.

The Ahmedabad Bombing

In November 1909, Lord Minto visited the city of Ahmedabad. As he and Lady Minto (who was also celebrating her birthday that day) were driving in a carriage with outriders, something was thrown towards them from the crowd. The security officials could not pin down what had been thrown, but subsequently two coconut bombs were discovered on the route of the Viceroy procession.

One of them exploded and dismembered the water-carrier's hand. Though nothing happened to the Viceregal couple, the incident became important as it was an attempt on the life of a Viceroy of India. Lady Minto is said to have later recorded in her journals that the bombs were 'a rather odd birthday gift'.

Looking back one can say that Indian nationalism, in many ways, was born out of the throes and woes of Bengal. And out of Bengal's agitation against the partition was born revolutionary terrorism. As Bengal's secret societies stirred violence and hatred against the British Government and its supporters, the tremors of Bengal now reached distant shores and banks. Secret societies were discovered in Central India and the Deccan and all evidence pointed to revolutionary terrorism gaining deep roots in northern India as well. Even distant London was not beyond the target-board of revolutionary activity. Madan Lal Dhingra proved it by shooting dead Sir William Curzon Wyllie, the Political ADC to the Secretary of State for India at the Imperial Institute in London on 1 July 1909. The tentacles of 'Bengal Terrorism' were indeed beginning to wear an inter-regional colour. The assassination of Jackson, the Collector of Nasik, on 21 December 1909 by Anant Laxman Kanhere was another pointer towards this.

Bengal, however, remained the heart of the movement. The relentless agitation, coupled with the bold actions of the revolutionary groups shook the very foundation of the British Government and ultimately contributed to its decision in 1911 to annul the partition of Bengal.

Lord Minto sailed back in 1910 and his troubled legacy was taken over by Lord Hardinge in November 1910. The 1909 Morley-Minto Reforms did seem to have temporarily softened some segments of Indian polity and society but on the whole it seemed that the British, and the new Governor-General, had come to terms with the fact that the partition of Bengal in 1905 had done more to fan the flames of Indian nationalism than fulfil the desired British political needs. The British realised that it was time to step back strategically. If only to jump a few steps forward ... .

Revocation of the Partition and Transfer of the Capital

On 22 June 1911, George V was crowned King at a glittering ceremony at the Westminster Abbey in London. In anticipation of George V's coronation, plans had already been afoot from early 1911 to organise a grand Coronation Durbar for the new King and Queen in Delhi in December. On 25 August 1911, driven by the opportunity as well as the need, the Government of India—in a highly confidential despatch to the Secretary of State for India—recommended major changes in the administrative structure of India, including the revocation of the partition of Bengal and the transfer of the capital of the British Indian empire

A view of the the sprawling camp-city set up for the grand Delhi Coronation Durbar in 1911

An imposing view of the spectacular Delhi Durbar

The royal procession on the occasion of the Delhi Durbar

from Calcutta to Delhi ... a city away from the hotbed of agitation, a city vantagely located, a city historically famed as a capital.

The crux of the despatch was that Delhi was to be made the imperial capital, with the city along with a part of the surrounding country under the direct administration of the Government of India. The five Bengali-speaking divisions—the Presidency, Burdwan, Dacca, Rajshahi and Chittagong—were to be united into a presidency of approximately 70,000 square miles, with a population of 42,000,000 administered by a Governor-in-Council. Bihar, Chota Nagpur and Orissa were to form a new province of approximately 113,000 square miles and a population of about 35,000,000 administered by a Lieutenant Governor-in-Council.

There would be a restoration of the Chief Commissionership for Assam, which would now administer an area of about 56,000 square miles and a population about 5,000,000.

Excerpts from a letter dated 25 August 1911, giving the reasoning behind the proposal to transfer the capital and reunify Bengal:

> My Lord Marquis,
>
> We shall, in the first place, attempt to set forth the circumstances which have induced us to frame these proposals at this particular juncture and then proceed to lay before your Lordship the broad general features of our scheme.
>
> That the Government of India should have its seat in the city as one of the chief Provincial Governments, and moreover in a city geographically so ill-adapted as Calcutta to be the capital of the Indian empire, has long been recognised to be a serious anomaly ... The considerations which explain its original selection as the principal seat of government have long since passed away with the consolidation of British rule throughout the peninsula and the development of a great inland system of railway communication ... .
>
> On the one hand, the almost incalculable importance of the part which can already safely be predicted for the Imperial Legislative Council, in the shape it has assumed under the Indian Councils Act of 1909, renders the removal of the capital to a more central and easily accessible position practically imperative. On the other hand, the peculiar political situation which has arisen in Bengal since the partition makes it eminently desirable to withdraw the Government of India from its present provincial environment ... .

Due to its location, historical importance and on the basis of political consideration the capital of the Indian empire should be at Delhi, and the announcement that the transfer of the seat of Government to Delhi had been sanctioned should be made by His Majesty, the King-Emperor, at the forthcoming Imperial Durbar in Delhi itself.

The maintenance of British rule in India depends on the ultimate supremacy of the Governor-General-in-Council and the Indian Councils Act of 1909 itself bears testimony to the impossibility of allowing matters of vital concern to be decided by a majority of non-official votes in the Imperial Legislative Council. Nevertheless it is certain that, in the course of time, the just demands of Indians for a larger share in the government of the country will have to be satisfied, and the question will be how this devolution of power can be conceded without impairing the supreme authority of the Governor-General-in-Council. The only possible solution of the difficulty would appear to be gradually to give the provinces a larger measure of self-government ... In order that this consummation may be attained, it is essential that the Supreme Government should not be associated with any particular Provincial Government ... It is generally recognised that the capital of a great Central Government should be separate and independent, and effect has been given to this principle in the United States, Canada and Australia.

The administrative advantages of the transfer would be scarcely less valuable than the political. In the first place, the development of the Legislative Councils has made the withdrawal of the Supreme Council and the Government of India from the influence of local opinion, a matter of ever-increasing urgency. Secondly, events in Bengal are apt to react on the Viceroy and the Government of India, to whom the responsibility for them is often wrongly attributed. The connection is bad for the Government of India, bad for the Bengal Government and unfair to the other provinces whose representatives view with great and increasing jealousy the predominance of Bengal. Further, public opinion in Calcutta is by no means always the same as that which obtains elsewhere in India, and it is undesirable that Government of India should be subject exclusively to its influence.

The question of providing a separate capital for the Government of India has often been debated, but generally with the object of finding a site where that Government could spend all seasons of the year. The Government of India would ... be able to stay in Delhi from 1 October to 1 May, whilst owing to the much greater proximity the annual migration to and from Shimla could be reduced in volume, would take up much less time and be far less costly. Some branches of the administration, such as Railways and Posts and Telegraphs, would obviously derive special benefit from the change to such a central position, and the only department which, as far as we can see, might be thought to suffer some inconvenience would be that of commerce and industry, which would be less closely in touch at Delhi with the commercial and industrial interests centred in Calcutta.

On the other hand, that department would be closer to the other commercial centres of Bombay and Karachi, whose interests are sometimes opposed to those of Calcutta and would thus be in a better position to deal impartially with the railways and commercial interests of the whole of India.

Delhi is still a name to conjure with. It is intimately associated in the minds of the Hindus with sacred legends that go back even beyond the dawn of history. It is in the plains of Delhi that the Pandava princes fought out with the Kauravas the epic struggle recorded in the Mahabharata and celebrated on the banks of the Yamuna the famous sacrifice that consecrated their title to the empire. The Purana Qila still marks the site of the city that they founded and called Indraprastha, barely three miles from the south gate of the modern city of Delhi. To the Mohammedans it would be a source of unbounded gratification to see the ancient capital of the Mughuls restored to its proud position as the seat of empire. Throughout India, as far south as the Mohammedan conquest extended, every walled town has its 'Delhi Gate', and among the masses of the people it is still revered as the seat of the former empire. The change would strike the imagination of the people of India as nothing else could do, would send a wave of enthusiasm throughout the country and would be accepted by all as the assertion of an unfaltering determination to maintain British rule in India … .

On Opposition from European Business Interests

The only serious opposition to the transfer that may be anticipated may, we think, come from the European commercial community of Calcutta, who might, we fear, not regard the creation of a Governorship of Bengal as altogether adequate compensation for the withdrawal of the Government of India. The opposition will be quite intelligible, but we can no doubt count upon their patriotism to reconcile them to a measure which would greatly contribute to the welfare of the Indian empire.

On the Reaction Expected from Bengalis

The Bengalis might not, of course, be favourably disposed to the proposal if it stood alone, for it will entail the loss of some of the influence that they now exercise owing to the fact that Calcutta is the headquarters of the Government of India. But as we hope presently to show, they should be reconciled to the change by other features of our scheme that are especially designed to give satisfaction to Bengali sentiments. In these circumstances we do not think that they would be so manifestly unreasonable as to oppose it, and if they did, might confidently expect that their opposition would raise no echo in the rest of India. Various circumstances have forced upon us the conviction that the bitterness of feelings engendered by the partition of Bengal is very widespread and unyielding and that we are by no means at an end of the troubles that have followed upon that measure. Eastern Bengal and Assam have, no doubt, benefitted greatly by the partition and the Mohammedans of that province, who form a large majority of the population, are loyal and contended, but the resentment among the Bengalis in both provinces—of Bengalis who hold most of the land, fill the professions and exercise a preponderating influence in public affairs—is as strong as ever, though somewhat less vocal.

The opposition to the Partition of Bengal was at first based mainly on sentimental grounds, but as we shall show later in discussing the proposed modification of the partition, since the enlargement of the Legislative Councils and especially of the representative element in them, the grievance of the Bengalis has become much more real and tangible and is likely to increase instead of to diminish. Everyone with any true desire for the peace and prosperity of this country must wish to find some manner of appeasement if it is in any way possible to do so. The simple rescission of the partition and a reversion to the status quo ante are manifestly impossible, both on political and on administrative grounds. The old province of Bengal was unmanageable under any form of government and we could not defraud the legitimate expectations of the Mohammedans of Eastern Bengal, who form the bulk of the population of that province and who have been loyal to the British Government throughout the trouble, without exposing ourselves to the charge of bad faith.

A settlement to be satisfactory and conclusive must provide convenient administration units; satisfy the legitimate aspirations of the Bengalis; duly safeguard the interests of the Mohammedans of Eastern Bengal and generally conciliate Mohammedan sentiment and be so clearly based upon broad grounds of political and administrative expediency as to negate any presumption that it has been exacted by clamour or agitation.

On Annulment as a Means to Alleviate Bengali Antagonism

The history of the Partition dates from 1902. Various schemes of territorial redistribution were at that time under consideration and that which was ultimately adopted had at any rate the merit of fulfilling two of the chief purposes that its authors had in view. It relieved the over-burdened administration of Bengal and it gave the Mohammedan population of Eastern Bengal advantages and opportunities of which they had perhaps hitherto not had their fair share.

On the other hand, as we have already pointed out, it was deeply resented by the Bengalis. No doubt sentiment has played a considerable part in the opposition offered by the Bengalis and, in saying this, we by no means wish to under-rate the importance that should be attached to sentiment even if it be exaggerated. It is, however, no longer a matter of mere sentiment but, rather, since the enlargement of the Legislative Councils, one of undeniable reality.

It has frequently been alleged in the press that the partition is the root cause of all recent troubles in India. The growth of political unrest in other parts of the country and notably in Dacca, before the partition of Bengal took place, disproves that assertion and we need not ascribe to the partition evils which have not obviously flowed from it. It is certain, however, that it is, in part of any rate, responsible for the growing estrangement that has now unfortunately assumed a very serious character in many parts of the country between Mohammedans and Hindus.

We are not without hope that a modification of the partition which we now propose will, in some degree at any rate, alleviate this most regrettable antagonism.

To sum up, the results anticipated from the partition have not been altogether realised and the scheme, as designed and executed, could only be justified by success. Although much good work has been done in Eastern Bengal and Assam and the Mohammedans of that province have reaped the benefits of a sympathetic administration closely in touch with them, those advantages have been in a great measure counterbalanced by the violent hostility that the partition has aroused among the Bengalis. For the reasons we have already indicated we feel bound to admit that the Bengalis are labouring under a sense of real injustice that we believe it would be sound policy to remove without further delay. The Durbar of December next affords a unique occasion for rectifying what is regarded by Bengalis as a grievous wrong.

The scheme that we have ventured to commend to Your Lordship's favourable consideration is not put forward with any spirit of opportunism, but in the belief that action on the lines proposed will be a bold stroke of statesmanship that would give unprecedented satisfaction and will forever associate so unique an event as the visit of the reigning sovereign of his Indian dominions with a new era in the history of India.

Excerpt from the General Sanction Given by the Secretary of State for India:

> I share in your belief that the transfer of the capital and the concomitant features of the scheme form a subject worthy of announcement by the King-Emperor in person on the unique and eagerly anticipated occasion at Delhi … .

The December 1911 Announcement by King George V:

> We are pleased to announce to our people that on the advice of our ministers, tendered after consultation with our Governor-General-in-Council, we have decided upon the transfer of the seat of the Government of India from Calcutta to the ancient capital of Delhi and, simultaneously, and as a consequence of that transfer, the creation at as early a date as possible, of a Governorship for the Presidency of Bengal, of a new Lieutenant Governorship-in-Council administering the areas of Bihar, Chota Nagpur and Orissa and of a Chief Commissionership of Assam, with such administrative changes and redistribution of boundaries as our Governor General-in-Council, with the approval of our Secretary of State for India-in-Council, may in due course determine … .

The government notification of 1912 that followed was one of the most important decisions in the history of British rule in India. Under the said notification, the 1905 division of Bengal was annulled and the capital of the Imperial Government was shifted to Delhi. The annulment was to come into effect on 1 April 1912. However, much before that, as the decision became known, the Muslims in the newly-formed province of Eastern Bengal and Assam felt let down by the British backtracking on the creation of a predominantly Muslim province after showing them a horizon full of promises. At the same time, the satisfaction of the predominantly Hindu Bengalis of the western part of Bengal, who had clamoured for annulment and fought for it, was dampened by the neutralising decision to shift the Indian capital from Calcutta to Delhi. From being an imperial capital, the city was now relegated to the stature of a provincial capital. This was bound to have a negative impact on real estate, enterprise and trade in the region.

Controversial, right since its ideation, the partition of Bengal was not free from controversy in its annulment too. Politically speaking, its inception had helped the government to create and fan Hindu-Muslim differences in the region. By giving the Muslims a distinct provincial identity, the British Government had subtly tried to diffuse a major Muslim participation in the Indian National Congress. It is also said that subsequently when the agitation against the partition was launched, many Muslims felt that the Congress was supporting an agitation against the creation of a Muslim majority province. Therefore, when the annulment came, most of the Muslims of the eastern part were very disappointed by the British turnaround. Many now felt that the British could not be trusted. This feeling was to have a bearing on future nationalist politics. Meanwhile, as anti-British feelings spread, Lord Hardinge, in a move to placate the East Bengali Muslim sentiment, promised a new University at Dacca. This step, in turn, invited echoes of protest from some quarters on the other side. It seemed that by now, the wedge that the British had driven through Bengal in 1905 was destined to keep the two parts distanced at many levels. The partition of 1905 that the 1912 proclamation only physically erased for the next few decades was destined to assume different incarnations in the years to come. History, after all, is a clock that is impossible to turn back. But Hardinge could be turned back ... at least that's what many thought, and resolved to achieve!

A bold attempt was made on the life of Viceroy Lord Hardinge

A Bomb for the Viceroy

In 1912 'Hardinge, Go Back!' became quite a popular slogan. And it was a slogan that wasn't confined to just Bengali voices. It was a slogan that cut across social and regional divides. In fact, it didn't remain a slogan confined to just voices and placards. In December 1912 in Delhi, 'Hardinge, Go Back!' was voiced in the form of a deafening bomb blast too. The tremors of 'Bengal Terrorism' had indeed travelled far.

Masterminded by Rash Behari Bose, a bold attempt was made on the life of Lord Hardinge as the Viceroy made his state entry into the new imperial capital sitting on a caparisoned elephant. As he was passing through the historic area of Chandni Chowk in Old Delhi, a bomb was hurled at him in the Dhulya Katra area. Hardinge had a narrow escape but was injured in the blast. In the chaos that followed the revolutionaries involved in throwing the bomb escaped. Rash Behari himself was a master of disguise and managed to elude the police dragnet that was laid out for them. An intense manhunt followed. Like the Muzaffarpur incident, the enquiries that followed revealed the existence of a deep revolutionary network.

Though the actual 'thrower' of the bomb was never conclusively identified, many people associated with the incident were arrested in due course and put on trial. Those who were convicted included Master Amir Chand, Avadh Bihari, Bal Mukund, Basanta Kumar Biswas of *Jugantar* and Lala Hanumant Sahai. The first four were sentenced to death. Master Amir Chand, Avadh Bihari and Bal Mukund were hanged in Delhi Jail on 8 May. Basant Kumar Biswas was hanged the next day at Ambala Jail. Rash Behari Bose later escaped to Japan, where he continued plotting against the British and was instrumental in the setting up of the Indian National Army that came to be led by the indomitable Subhas Chandra Bose.

The Disappearing Pistols

While the sentencing of top leaders left many groups in temporary disarray, it is also equally true that every imprisonment, every transportation order, every death sentence spawned new revolutionaries and groups committed to sacrifice their lives for the country by carrying on the fight. But to do so they needed funds and arms and this need they fulfilled by a variety of means. One of the most sensational arms thefts in Bengal happened just a month after the outbreak of World War I in Europe.

It was Wednesday, 26 August 1914. A clerk of Rodda & Company (a firm of gun makers in Calcutta) was sent to clear the import of 202 cases of arms and ammunition from the Customs House. He came back with 192 cases to the company's warehouse and then, saying that he was leaving to fetch the remainder, the clerk never returned. After three days the case was reported to the police. The 10 missing boxes contained 50 Mauser pistols (.300 bore) and 46,000 rounds of Mauser ammunition for them.

The pistols were quite unique because the box that contained the pistol was designed to fit the butt and convert the weapon from a handheld pistol to a shoulder-fired gun. Rodda & Company had a record of the

The famous Mauser pistol and its twin-utility carrying case

The Mauser pistol with its carrying case doubling up for use as a rifle butt

serial number of each pistol. A search began. Intelligence authorities discovered that 44 of them had been immediately distributed among nine revolutionary groups in Bengal.

The police later estimated that they were used in about 54 cases. In due course, 31 pistols were recovered from various parts of Bengal. One can hazard a guess that as more and more secret societies came up all over the country in the first half of the 20th century, many of the 19 Mausers that were not found must have continued to create a lot trouble for the British.

The Movement After World War I

Much to British discomfort, the revolutionaries now stepped up their activities all over the country. The network of secret societies was much bigger, the participatory base was much more heterogeneous and the targets bolder and more varied as well. With this widening of the revolutionary base, differences in modus operandi and beliefs were also bound to emerge.

The Dacca Anushilan Samiti and *Jugantar* differed on issues such as the 'Indo-German Plot' in which some revolutionaries were able to make contact with the German Foreign Office for the supply of arms and funds during World War I.

Though *Jugantar* managed to get some money, the attempt to smuggle arms into the country ended in failure as the shipload (purchased through a German agent) was seized in the U.S.A. In India, the famous revolutionary leader 'Bagha' Jatin died fighting in September 1915—trapped by the British Police while waiting for the arms.

To curb wartime revolutionary activity, the Defence of India Act was passed in 1915, giving the government extraordinary powers to have suspects tried by special tribunals against whose decisions there could be no appeal.

These emergency powers were later extended by the more sweeping reach of the Rowlatt Act of 1918. Protests against the Act culminated in the massacre of hundreds of innocent people by the British Indian Army at Jallianwala Bagh on Baisakhi (the traditional New Year Day in Punjab) on 13 April 1919, under the command of Brigadier General Reginald Dyer—more imfamously known as 'The Butcher of Amritsar'.

The massacre resulted in many violent reactions. It also paved the way for the launch of the first non-cooperation movement by Mahatma Gandhi.

Differences arose between *Jugantar* and the Dacca Anushilan Samiti on the question of support to Gandhi's non-cooperation movement. While *Jugantar* was agreeable to the request to temporarily suspend revolutionary action, the Dacca Anushilan Samiti refused to stop its activities but did not undertake any major attacks.

With the suspension of the non-cooperation movement in 1922, both groups resumed revolutionary activities with a major burst. Surya Sen made his famous raid on the Chittagong office of the Assam-Bengal Railway in December 1923. As revolutionary activity spawned once again in Bengal, the Bengal Criminal Law Amendment Ordinance was passed in 1924. It was extended as an Act in 1925 and, armed with its special powers, the police imprisoned almost 200 suspects between 1924 and 1927.

Calcutta to Lahore via Varanasi

Meanwhile, a group linked with Bengal revolutionaries was established in Varanasi by Sachindranath Sanyal, Jogesh Chatterjee and others. Known as the Hindustan Republican Association, it included Chandrashekhar Azad, Ramprasad Bismil, Ashfaqullah Khan and Rajendra Lahiri and its network extended from Calcutta to Lahore. The group carried out the sensational looting of government money in the famous Kakori Train Robbery on 11 August 1925. Ashfaqullah Khan, Ramprasad Bismil, Rajendra Lahiri and Roshan Singh were hanged for the act. The group later redefined itself into the Hindustan Socialist Republican Association and included Batukeshwar Dutt, Bhagat Singh, Sukhdev and Rajguru. Batukeshwar Dutt and Bhagat Singh were arrested for throwing a bomb in the Central Assembly in Delhi on 8 April 1929. Along with Sukhdev and Rajguru, Bhagat Singh was later charged with the murder of police officer J.P. Saunders and hanged in Lahore on 23 May 1931—less than a month after Azad had shot himself in Allahabad, with the last bullet left in his revolver, to avoid falling into the hands of the British Police that had surrounded him after a long gunfight.

Meanwhile, even as Mahatma Gandhi launched the nationwide civil disobedience movement with his salt *satyagraha*, back in Bengal, Surya Sen and his team, which included two women revolutionaries, Pritilata Waddedar and Kalpana Dutta, raided the Chittagong Armoury on

18 April 1930. Some died in the attack and of those who were later arrested, 12 were sentenced to transportation for life.

Betrayed by a colleague, Surya Sen was put on trial and hanged to death on 8 January 1934. This was perhaps the last great outburst of the revolutionary movement in Bengal.

The Eternal Stand

From Calcutta to Lahore, from Lahore to London ... the chain of revolutionary events was, in many ways, an echo of that first bomb hurled by Khudiram Bose and Prafulla Chaki at Muzaffarpur on 30 April 1908 on what they presumed to be Douglas Kingsford's carriage. Since then, wherever bullets were fired, wherever bombs were hurled, there was always a little bit of 'Alipore' in it.

Like all other historical phenomena, this revolutionary outburst was a product of its times. As times changed, political demands impacted the choice of strategies. The revolutionary stream gradually merged into the mainstream of nationalist politics. Tempered by fire, the true revolutionary, however, always stayed a revolutionary at heart, regardless of whichever party, organisation or activity that he or she became affiliated to.

Heroic, inspired, courageous, emotional and, at times, quite recklessly brave, the revolutionaries made an unforgettable contribution to the growth of the nationalist spirit in India. As one historian puts it, "They gave us back the pride of our manhood." Of course, we can never forget that they included some of the bravest women too! And neither can we forget that it was their ever-active, fiery presence that actually compelled the British Government to deal more seriously with the leaders of the non-violent, legally founded, nationalist political parties, especially the Indian National Congress. The other option—of dealing with revolutionaries and protracted revolutionary violence—was much more difficult for the British.

Indeed, the crude bomb that was hurled on that significant day in 1908 had its reverbations in history; its repercussions have impacted the lives of every Indian.

Epilogue

This story almost did not happen. Or at least all evidence of the proceedings could well have been obliterated. For, the records—the bundles of documents and files pertaining to the Alipore Bomb Conspiracy Case—were marked for destruction in 1936. They were supposed to be sold to a wastepaper dealer.

The then record-keeper, Mr. Jitendra Nath Ghose Dostidar, however, approached senior lawyer Mr. C.B. Banerjee and requested him to take some steps for the preservation of these invaluable records. Subsequently, Mr. Banerjee went to Mr. Ellis, the District Judge at that time, and appealed to him to stop the destruction of these records. Mr. Ellis advised the record-keeper to indicate that the records were destroyed and requested him to place them in a corner of the record room.

Thus, the records remained there unofficially for more than 12 years. In 1949, they were eventually rescued from dusty oblivion and transferred to a steel cupboard, especially provided in the judge's own retiring room. They remained there for almost 47 years.

In 1997, it was proposed that the records of the historic trial that took place in the Alipore District Court be exhibited, to coincide with the celebration of the Golden Jubilee of India's Independence. Mr. P.L. Dutta, the then Chief Judge, City Civil and Sessions Court, Calcutta, made considerable efforts to locate the records, along with several other valuable case records. They were unable to open the cupboard that was kept in Nazarath at the Alipore Court and had to take the help of a petty thief. The entire files were finally located and put on public display.

The Key Players in the Case

Aurobindo Ghose

Aurobindo Ghose, better known as Sri Aurobindo, was born in Kolkata (Calcutta) on 15 August 1872 to Dr. Krishnadhone Ghose and Swarnalata Devi. His father, Krishnadhone Ghose (1845-1893), belonged to the well-known Ghose family of Konnagar, West Bengal. Dr. Ghose had lived in Britain and had studied at the Aberdeen University. He was determined that his children should also have a completely European upbringing. In fact, even the name given to Aurobindo at birth was Aurobindo 'Akroyd' Ghose, because during his birth an English lady named Annette Akroyd was a guest of his parents. Aurobindo and his siblings were first sent to the Loreto Convent School at Darjeeling and then, at the age of seven, Aurobindo was taken along with his elder brothers Manamohan and Benoybhushan to England.

There they were placed under the care of a clergyman and his wife, Reverend and Mrs. Drewett, at Manchester. The couple tutored Aurobindo privately. Aurobindo was then admitted to the St. Paul's School in London as a scholar. By now he had already learnt Latin, and read Shakespeare and the Romantic poets on his own. Aurobindo went on to master Greek and Latin at school and his last three years at St. Paul's were spent in reading, among other subjects, a lot of English poetry. A brilliant student, at St. Paul's he received the Butterworth Prize for Literature, the Bedford Prize for History and a scholarship to King's College, Cambridge University.

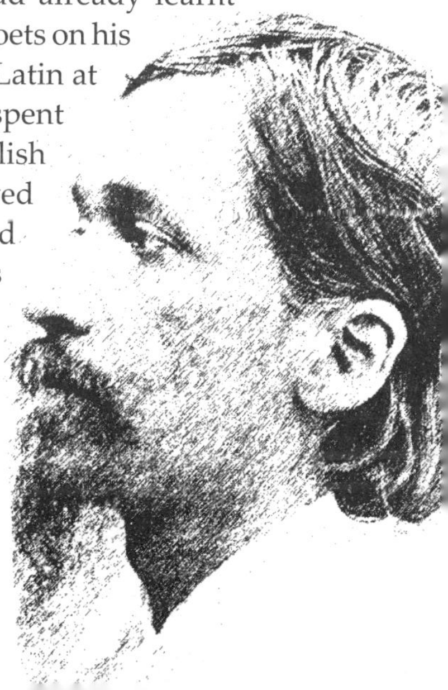

Interestingly, Judge C.P. Beachcroft who tried Sri Aurobindo in the Alipore Bomb Conspiracy Case was his co-student at Cambridge. Aurobindo started writing poetry in Greek, Latin and English and later took up literary

Bengali too. As secretary to the Indian Majlis, Cambridge University, he made revolutionary speeches that hinted at armed rebellion as the way to India's liberation. In 1890 Aurobindo passed the open competition for the Indian Civil Service. However, at the end of two years of probation, he failed to present himself at the horse-riding test and was disqualified for the service.

After 14 years in England, Aurobindo returned to India in 1893 and was appointed to the Baroda State Service where he worked in the revenue department, the Maharaja's Secretariat, then as Professor of English and finally as Acting Principal of the Baroda College. While in Baroda, he learnt Sanskrit, Marathi, Gujarati and Bengali; studied the epics, the Upanishads as well as Sanskrit literature and wrote poetry, plays and essays in English. In 1901, Aurobindo married Mrinalini Devi (1888-1918).

During the partition of Bengal in 1905, he became a leader of the group of Indian nationalists who came to be known as extremists for their willingness to use violence and their advocacy of outright independence. In 1906, during the peak of the *swadeshi* and boycott movements, he was elected to be the Principal of the National College at Calcutta. Meanwhile he continued writing and publishing bold articles to stir the spirit of nationalism through *Bande Mataram*, a fiery Bengali newspaper that he edited. In 1907, Aurobindo was prosecuted for seditious writing, but acquitted for lack of substantial evidence. In 1908, he was arrested again—this time in connection with the Alipore Bomb Conspiracy Case—and imprisoned for a year in the Alipore Jail in Calcutta.

While incarcerated at Alipore, he embarked on a contemplative journey, meditated on scriptures such as the *Bhagavad Gita* and underwent a remarkable transformation that made him see compassion, honesty and charity even in the hearts of murderers. After his acquittal in 1909, Aurobindo resumed his work with two newly started weeklies, *Karmayogin* in English and *Dharma* in Bengali, in both of which he wrote articles on the deeper significance of Indian nationalism. In February 1910, he received information that his office was going to be searched and that he would be arrested again. Aurobindo was advised to leave for Chandernagore. From there Aurobindo went to Pondicherry. At Pondicherry he completely withdrew from political activities and devoted himself entirely to spirituality, philosophy and literature. In this work, he received the support of Mirra Richard (later known as the Mother), who settled in Pondicherry in 1920 and was instrumental in establishing the Aurobindo Ashram. Sri Aurobindo, as the world calls him today, retired into seclusion at the Ashram and maintained it till his death in 1950. His major spiritual and philosophical works include *The Life Divine, The Synthesis of Yoga, The Ideal of Human Unity, The Human Cycle, The Foundations of Indian Culture, The Secret of the Veda* and *Savitri*—his magnum opus in poetry.

Barindra Kumar Ghose

Barindra Kumar Ghose, popularly known as Barin Ghose, was born in Croydon (Norwood) near London on 5 January 1880. One of the founder members of Jugantar, the famous revolutionary secret society that fired the imagination of the youth of Bengal in the first three decades of the 20th century, Barin Ghose was the younger brother of Aurobindo Ghose.

It was the influence of Aurobindo that drew Barin Ghose into the heart of India's nationalist struggle against British imperialism in the first decade of the 20th century. Barin Ghose did his high school from Deoghar and later enrolled at the Patna College. However, drawn by the pull of the times, Barin moved to Baroda, where he learnt rifle-shooting. Subsequently he moved to Calcutta and began organising the revolutionary groups into a powerful network.

Barin also started publishing *Jugantar*, a Bengali weekly, and was instrumental in establishing a revolutionary organisation also called Jugantar, consisting of members from the inner circle of the Anushilan Samiti. A torchbearer of what came to be feared by the British as 'Bengal Terrorism', Barin Ghose's famous Maniktola Group of revolutionaries operated from a secret location at Maniktola in Kolkata where they manufactured bombs and collected arms and ammunition.

After the attempt on the life of Douglas Kingsford at Muzaffarpur by Khudiram Bose and Prafulla Chaki, police investigation led to the arrest of Barin Ghose along with many of his comrades. The trial—the Alipore Bomb Conspiracy Case—sentenced Barin Ghose to death. However, the sentence was reduced to life imprisonment and Barin was deported to the Cellular Jail in the

Andaman Islands. Released in 1920, after the British granted amnesty to many following World War I, he returned to Kolkata and started a career in journalism. Influenced by the spiritual teachings of Aurobindo, he left for Pondicherry in 1923 but returned to Kolkata in 1929 and again took to journalism. He was associated with the newspaper *The Statesman* and was later the editor of the Bengali daily *Basumati*. Barindra Ghose died on 18 April 1959.

Chittaranjan Das

Born on 5 November 1870, Chittaranjan Das had his early education in the London Missionary Society Institution at Bhowanipur and graduated from Presidency College, Kolkata, in 1890. He then proceeded to England where he joined the Middle Temple and was called to the Bar in 1892. Returning to India in 1893, he enrolled himself at the Bar of the Calcutta High Court. A series of sensational criminal and civil cases in which he used his vast knowledge of British law and great legal acumen established his reputation as a brilliant lawyer. These included his famous defence of Aurobindo Ghose in the Alipore Bomb Conspiracy Case. It was his intelligent defence that proved instrumental in getting the acquittal of Aurobindo Ghose.

At the height of his legal career Chittaranjan Das gave up legal practice to devote all his energies to India's struggle for freedom. Along with Motilal Nehru, he founded the Swaraj Party to give a strong platform to its non-liberal opinions. A leading figure in Bengal during the non-cooperation movement of 1919-1922, throughout his political life he displayed great courage and determination in raising his voice and demands in the face of the British. Endearingly called 'Desh Bandhu' (friend of the country), the brilliant barrister, poet, social worker and nationalist leader died on 16 June 1925.

Ullaskar Dutt

Ullaskar Dutt was born on 16 April 1885 in the Kalikachha village in the Brahmanbaria district of present-day Bangladesh. A degree holder in agriculture from the London University, Ullaskar also studied at the Presidency College in Kolkata. He was rusticated from the college for

hitting Professor Russell, a British professor who had passed some derogatory comments about Bengalis. A member of the Jugantar party, he was an expert bomb-maker. It was a bomb made by him and Hem Chandra Das that Khudiram Bose and Prafulla Chaki used in their attempt to murder Kingsford at Muzaffarpur in 1908. Ullaskar was arrested with his compatriots after the Muzaffarpur incident.

Along with Barin Ghose, Ullaskar Dutt was sentenced to death by hanging in the Alipore Bomb Conspiracy Case. The sentence was later reduced to transportation for life at the Cellular Jail in the Andamans. Ullaskar was subjected to brutal torture in jail and is said to have lost his mental balance. For days he was hung by his wrists from a peg hammered into the wall above his head. It is said that in a handwritten letter sent in June 1912, Harold Wheeler, Secretary to the Government of India, wrote to Sir Reginald Craddock, Home Member, Governor General's Council; "I am inclined to think that the punishment of standing handcuffs is brutal and it would be well to inquire the desirability of its continuance." Sir Reginald is said to have replied, "Handcuffing to a staple is in my experience as effective on the recalcitrant as flogging. It undoubtedly causes great discomfort but Ullaskar Dutt is nothing more than a murderer and it seems to me a mistaken indulgence that he was not hanged."

Ullaskar Dutt was set free in 1920. He returned to Kolkata but was arrested again in 1931 and sentenced to 18 months of imprisonment. When the British rule ended in 1947, Ullaskar returned to his home village in Brahmanbaria (which had become a part of East Pakistan) only to live a lonely life for 10 years. He returned to Kolkata in 1957 and his last years were spent in Silchar. Ullaskar Dutt died on 17 May 1965.

Khudiram Bose

Khudiram Bose was born on 3 December 1889 in Bhuvaini village in the Medinipur (Midnapur) district of Bengal. His father Trailokyanath Bose was a *tahsildar*.

His mother's name was Lakshmipriya Devi. Inspired by his readings of the *Bhagavad Gita*, Khudiram decided to join Jugantar, one of the leading secret societies of his time and undertake revolutionary activities to end British rule in India.

Emotionally moved at the young age of 16 by the partition of Bengal, Khudiram Bose found himself drawn to defying the police, distributing nationalist literature and helping the senior revolutionaries of the group in various activities.

Along with Prafulla Chaki, Khudiram Bose was sent to Muzaffarpur in Bihar to assassinate Kingsford, the ex-Magistrate of Calcutta Presidency, posted as District Judge of Muzaffarpur.

On the evening of 30 April 1908, the duo waited in front of the gate of station club at Muzaffarpur and hurled a bomb at a carriage that they thought was carrying Kingsford. Unfortunately, the vehicle was carrying two innocent British ladies—the wife and daughter of Barrister Pringle Kennedy. Both of them were killed. In the manhunt that followed, Prafulla Chaki committed suicide and Khudiram was arrested.

Put on trial, Khudiram Bose was sentenced to death and hanged on 11 August 1908 at the age of 19. His execution sparked an irreversible chain reaction of events in India's struggle for freedom from British rule.

ফাঁসী

একবার বিদায় দে মা
ঘুরে আসি,
হাসি হাসি পরবো ফাঁসী
দেখবে ভারতবাসী।

একবার বিদায় দে মা
ঘুরে আসি

কলের বোমা তৈরী করে
দাঁড়িয়ে ছিলেম রাস্তার ধারে,
বড়লাটকে মারতে গিয়ে
মারলাম আর এক ইংল্যান্ডবাসী।

একবার বিদায় দে মা
ঘুরে আসি

শনিবার বেলা দশটার পরে
জজকোর্টেতে লোক না ধরে, মাগো।
হলো অভিরামের দ্বীপ চালান মা,
ক্ষুদিরামের ফাঁসী।

একবার বিদায় দে মা
ঘুরে আসি

বারো লক্ষ তেত্রিশ কোটী
রইল মা তোর ব্যাটা বেটি, মাগো
তাদের নিয়ে ঘর করিস মা,
বউদের করিস দাসী।

একবার বিদায় দে মা
ঘুরে আসি

দশমাস দশদিন পরে
জন্ম নেবো মাসীর ঘরে, মাগো
তখন যদি না চিনতে পারিস
দেখবি গলায় ফাঁসী।

একবার বিদায় দে মা
ঘুরে আসি

পীতাম্বর দাস।

Phaanshi

Ek baar bidai de Ma, ghure aashi,
Haashi Haashi, porbo phaanshi
Dekhbe Bharatbaashi.

Ek baar bidai de Ma, ghure aashi.

Koler boma toiri kore,
Dariye chhilaam rastaar dhaare, Mago;
Boro Laat ke marte giye,
Marlaam aar ek Englandbaashi.

Ek baar bidai de Ma, ghure aashi.

Shonibaar bela doshtaar pore,
Judge courte te lok na dhore Mago;
Hogo Abhiramer dwip chalan, Ma
Khudiramer phaanshi.

Ek baar bidai de Ma, ghure aashi.

Baro lokkho tetrish koti,
Roilo Ma tor beta beti, Mago;
Tader niye ghor korish, Ma
Bowder korish daashi.

Ek baar bidai de Ma, ghure aashi.

Dosh mash dosh din pore,
Jonmo nebo Maashir ghore, Mago;
Tokhon jodi na chinte parish,
Dekhbi golai phaanshi.

Ek baar bidai de Ma, ghure aashi.

The Noose

Bid me farewell for once, Mother,
I shall return.
The people of India will see
How I slip on the noose with a smile ever on my face.

Bid me farewell for once, Mother,
I shall return.

With a crude bomb in hand
I was standing by the roadside;
In our bid to assassinate the district judge
We ended up killing another Englishman.

Bid me farewell for once, Mother,
I shall return.

On Saturday morning, after 10 o' clock,
The courtroom was bursting with people, O Mother;
Abhiram was to be sent to the Andamans
And Khudiram to be hanged.

Bid me farewell for once, Mother,
I shall return.

You will still have your thirty crore
And twelve lakh sons and daughters;
Make your home with them, O Mother,
Let the brides be your handmaidens.

Bid me farewell for once, Mother,
I shall return.

Ten months ten days hence,
I shall be born to your sister;
If then you fail to recognize me,
Look for the noose around my neck.

Bid me farewell for once, Mother,
I shall return.

Bibliography

– Agarwala, B.R., *Trials of Independence*, NBT, New Delhi, 1991.

– Bose, Bejoy Krishna, *The Alipore Bomb Trial*, Butterworth & Co. India Ltd., London, 1922.

– Buchan, John, *Lord Minto, A Memoir*, 1924.

– Dalley, Jan, *The Black Hole: Money, Myth and Empire*, Fig Tree, London, June, 2006.

– Darnton, Robert, *Literary Surveillance in the British Raj: The Contradictions of Liberal Imperialism*, Volume 4, 2001, Penn State University Press.

– Dirles, Nichols, *Scandal of the Empire—India and the Creation of Imperial Britain*, Harvard University Press, London, 2006.

– Findlay, *Nur Jahan*, Oxford University Press.

– Furedy, Chris, *Lord Curzon and the Reform of the Calcutta Corporation 1889: A Case Study in Imperial Decision Making*, York University Press.

– Hill, B.C., *The Indian Record Series, Bengal in 1756-7*, 3 volumes, London.

– Majumdar, R.C., Ray Chaudhury, H.C. and Datta, K., *An Advanced History of India*, Macmillan India, Madras, 1978.

– Marshall, P.J., *Bengal—The British Bridgehead*, Cambridge, 1987.

– *Freedom Struggle*, NBT, New Delhi, 1972.

– Pal, Bipin Chandra, *India's Struggle for Independence 1857-1947*. Penguin, New Delhi, 1988.

– Perinue, J., *History of Universe*, Paris, 1950.

– Spear, Percival, *Master of Bengal: Clive and His India*, London, 1975.

– Sir Raleigh, J., *Lord Curzon in India*.

– Spear, Percival, *A History of India*, Penguin Books, 1977.

– Ed. Sarkar, Jadunath, *The Later Mughals* by William Irvine, D.K. Publishers Distributors Pvt. Ltd., Delhi, 1995.

- Ed. Roshan and Apurva, *Sri Aurobindo in Baroda*, Sri Aurobindo Ashram, Pondicherry, 1993.
- Sri Aurobindo, *Bande Mataram—Writing of Sri Aurobindo Ghose*, Aurobindo Ashram, Pondicherry.
- Justice Rowlatt, *The Revolutionary History of India—Sedition Committee 1918*, New Age Publishers Pvt. Ltd., Calcutta, 1918.
- F. No. 104-111, Year 1908; National Archives, Month May, *Proposed Deportation of Aurobindo Ghose, Abinash Chandra Bhattacharji and Sailendra Kumar Bose Under Regulation 1616 of 1818.*
- F. No 112-150, Year 1908; National Archives, Month May, *Bomb Outrage at Muzaffarpur, Discovery of Bombs, etc., and an Anarchist Plot in Calcutta.*
- F. No 17-21, National Archives *Explosion of Bomb in Gujarat,* Calcutta, June 1908.
- F. No 34-37, National Archives *Prosecution of the* Bande Mataram *Newspapers,* January 1908.
- *Bengal Regulation III of 1818.*
- F. No 106-116, National Archives *Bomb Found on the Steps of St. Andrew's Church,* 26 Upper Circular Road, Calcutta, June 1908.
- F. No 130-131, National Archives *Report on the Events Prior and Subsequent to the Bomb Outrage at Muzaffarpur,* June 1908.
- F. No 134-136, *Result of the Prosecution in the Muzaffarpur Bomb Outrage Case,* June 1908.
- F. No 54; *Bengal Report Regarding the Bomb Explosion in Grey Street, Calcutta,* July 1908.
- F. No. 137-139 *Interception of Copies of the Publication as the Circular of Freedom,* July 1908.
- F. No 18-24, *Prosecution of Atul Kumar Pal Under the Explosive Substances Act 1908 for Sending a Parcel Containing a Bomb to the District Magistrate, Nadia,* October 1908.
- F. No. 28-32, *Bomb Explosion Near Sharanagar and Discovery of Two Bombs Near the Railway Line at Chandernagore,* December 1908.
- Roy Chowdhury, Jitendra Nath, F. No 37, *Attempted Assassination of Sir Andrew Fraser, Lt. Governor of Bengal* by the Young Men's Christian Association, Over Town Hall, Calcutta, 41A, December 1908.
- Proceedings of the Home Department, December 1911, Pro No. 10 Transfer of seat of Govt. of India from Calcutta to Delhi, State Archives.
- F. No. 6 of 1905, Government of India, Home Department, State Archives.
- Trial of Khudiram Bose, Case No. 66408 of 1908 in folder - Vol. III.

— Trial of Khudiram Bose, Case No. 66408 of 1908, Vol. II.

— Trial of Khudiram Bose, Case No. 66408 of 1908, Vol. IV.

— Crown v/s Khudiram Bose. Case No. 66408 of 1908, Vol. I.

— Crown v/s Khudi Ram Bose & others, Case No. 66408 of 1908, Vol. VI.

— Case against Aurobindo Ghose, F. No. 205/1909, State Archives.

— Case against Aurobindo Ghose, F. No. 205/1909, State Archives.

— F. No. 24/1909, State Archives.

— Alipore Bomb Case F. No. 194/1909, State Archives.

— Emperor v/s B.K. Ghose & others, 1908, Calcutta.